William Maskell, Museum South Kensington

The Industrial Arts

historical sketches with numerous illustrations - published for the Committee of

Council on Education

William Maskell, Museum South Kensington

The Industrial Arts
historical sketches with numerous illustrations - published for the Committee of Council on Education

ISBN/EAN: 9783337095932

Printed in Europe, USA, Canada, Australia, Japan

Cover: Foto ©Thomas Meinert / pixelio.de

More available books at **www.hansebooks.com**

THE INDUSTRIAL ARTS
HISTORICAL SKETCHES
WITH NUMEROUS
ILLUSTRATIONS

Published for the Committee of Council on Education

BY

CHAPMAN AND HALL, 193, PICCADILLY

PREFACE.

These sketches are intended to supply, and especially for the use of those who know but little, some general information with regard to the history of the chief classes or divisions of art-workmanship. We know that many valuable books, and papers or articles in cyclopædias and serial publications, have been already written upon the same subjects: but they are not readily to be referred to when examining the collections themselves, and are often too expensive to be within the reach of the majority of people. The present little volume will meet, we hope, both these difficulties.

The South Kensington museum, including the time when the collections were first exhibited at Marlborough House, has now been open to the public for very nearly a quarter of a century. It is scarcely possible to estimate the amount of influence for good which has been already exercised over the art productions of English workmen: and this has been widely owned, not only at home but abroad. Thousands upon thousands have every year passed through the galleries and courts; and even those who have come solely from an idle curiosity must have carried away with them the knowledge of very much about which they had hitherto been utterly ignorant. In many cases also an interest has been created which did not before exist, and naturally that interest would be followed by a desire to see the collections again and to learn more about them.

Many a man, ignorant of what is in him, may be strolling through the museum simply to fill up a vacant half-hour; and his eye falling upon some object of particular importance to himself he will have reason to look back with gratitude to the results of that accidental visit. A thought may strike him,—in the way of some improvement in a mechanical process, or of some application of artistic decoration not yet attempted,—and new ideas may be roused, or energy given to dormant powers, of the nature of which he was perhaps not even aware.

The main benefit to be expected from the public exhibition of such collections as that at South Kensington is a higher average of knowledge among people generally. We must not look for too much; nor must we be disappointed if year after year pass by, and we are still unable to name an English rival of Michael Angelo, or della Robbia, Cellini, or Bernard Palissy. We might as well complain that the enormous increase of schools in the last thirty years has not produced a Dante, Shakespeare, or Bacon. Capability to attain eminent excellence springs from genius, and genius is rare. Men who are not of their own time only but of all time, and whose names are household words in every quarter of the world, are very few in number: and they must be born with power to reach the topmost rank. This is true of every kind of art or workmanship; and may be illustrated by the example, seen every day, of those who amuse themselves with common games. No amount of practice, no observation of the skill of others, will enable any one to go beyond a certain limit: and Deschapelles at whist or Philidor at chess were as unapproachable in their own way as the great artists of *antiquity or the middle ages in sculpture or painting or enamelling. Mental endowments, or what we usually call talent, belong in various degrees to all men: and rightly to teach, to guide, and, above all, to stimulate these is the great object of art collections. For talent requires to be stimulated, excited, and spurred on to work: genius, on the contrary, may call for guidance, may gain from exercise, but cannot, if it would, be idle.*

The collections at South Kensington include large numbers of objects in each class, giving not only examples but in some cases almost the history also of the particular art itself; among them are not a few of the very best and finest specimens known to exist. In more than one series the collection rivals any other either in England or abroad: and the student may trace their progress—for example, of Ivories from the first century, of Textiles from the middle ages, of Pottery from the sixteenth century—down to our own day. Large sums have been well expended in procuring the best specimens. The eye requires education, and a degree of teaching which inferior things fail to supply. Ignorant or ill-informed people commonly admire and express approval of objects which are "second class" or even lower. Experience and observation will alone enable any man—and this only slowly and by patient steps—to judge rightly what is best and in the truest taste or style.

Already we may observe a great change in public opinion and judgment as to what is really good. We no longer hear approval of the coarse and ugly works of art (so called) which were admired some fifty or sixty years ago. It must be in some very remote district that even poor people would now buy for the shelves of a cottage the hideous "ornaments" which were at that time the only decorations within their reach.

The compiler of this little book—for it is scarcely more than a mere compilation—felt grave doubts as to undertaking it at all: nor are these diminished now that it is finished. The space allowed is extremely limited, and the difficulty was to know how little to say; that little, also, to be as useful as might be upon a dozen different subjects. He feels how much information has been omitted which many, better competent than himself to judge, will think should have been included; and, on the other hand, how much may properly have been left out as unnecessary or trivial. But he must be content, and set it against what he would own to be just criticism, if any who were altogether ignorant before shall acquire knowledge, small though it may be, some upon one subject and some upon another. The book is not meant for learned people: the object of it is to give the "commonest information;" information (as we say) to be found anywhere. This, however, is frequently that which is most widely wanted, and very seldom at hand.

No notes or references to authorities are added: these authorities and larger works entering far more widely into details may easily be obtained by every one who desires to enquire further. Moreover, many of the following pages would have merely contained, over and over again, constant references to, and marks of quotation from, such books (for example) as the admirable works of Sir Digby Wyatt upon mosaics, or Mr. Nesbitt upon glass. The article upon lace is a reprint of Mrs. Palliser's introduction to the catalogue of the South Kensington collection.

W. M.

April, 1876.

CONTENTS.

	PAGE
Gold and silver work	1
Bronze, copper, and iron	33
Enamels	51
Furniture	69
Ivories	93
Pottery and porcelain	117
Maiolica	161
Glass	187
Mosaics	211
Arms and armour	227
Textile fabrics	239
Lace	257

LIST OF WOODCUTS.

		PAGE
Portion of antique mosaic, found in Rome		*Frontispiece*
Interior of mediæval goldsmith's shop		xv
The golden candlestick		3
Silver tray from Hildesheim		8
5 Outside of cup from Hildesheim		9
Interior of same cup		9
Votive crown of king Suintila		11
Gaulish armlet		12
Crown of Charlemagne		13
10 Golden altar from Basle		14
Shrine, twelfth century		16
The coronation spoon		16
The coronation "ampulla"		17
Anne Boleyn's sceptre		19
15 .Chalice, French		20
„ „		20
„ German		20
„ Spanish		20
„ Italian		21
20 „ English		21
„ German		21
„ „		21
Scent box, sixteenth century		22
Pendant, fifteenth century		23
25 „ attributed to Cellini		24
Cup, lapis lazuli		26
„ rock crystal		26
English sugar sifter, 1580		26
Basin, English, 1684		26
30 Augsburg cup, 1600		27
English cup, 1611		27
English tankard, 1650		27
Cup and cover, English, 1660		27
Salver, Flemish, 1670		28
35 Tankard, Nuremberg, 1650		28

THE INDUSTRIAL ARTS.

		PAGE
Cup, English, 1710		29
Tureen „ 1773		29
Kettle „ 1732		30
Vase „ 1770		30
40 Table „ 1700		30
Pendant, with diamonds		32
Censer, metal; twelfth century		33
Hanging lamp; ninth century		40
The bell of St. Patrick		41
45 Bell; twelfth century		41
Dove; thirteenth century		42
Crozier; thirteenth century		43
Cup and cover		44
Candlestick; Italian, sixteenth century		44
50 Lamp stand; Italian, sixteenth century		45
Small metal shrine; Italian, sixteenth century		46
Milanese dagger		47
Iron bolt		48
„ French		48
55 Key; fifteenth century		49
„ fifteenth century		50
Base of Limoges salt-cellar		51
Altar tray and chalice		55
Byzantine reliquary		56
60 Cup, with translucent enamels		59
Champlevé enamel: fourteenth century		60
Shrine; thirteenth century		61
Portable altar; thirteenth century		62
Vase, Limoges; sixteenth century		65
65 Parts of a salt-cellar, Pierre Raymond		66
Candlestick, Battersea enamel		68
Royal dinner table, fourteenth century		69
Stool, Assyrian		72
Chair „		72
70 Greek chairs		73
„ couches		73
Roman tripod		74
„ candelabrum		74
„ couch		74
75 Chair of St. Peter		75
„ of Dagobert		76
Bedstead, eleventh century		76
Seats, fourteenth century		77

		PAGE
	Bedroom, fourteenth century	77
80	Round table, fourteenth century	78
	The coronation chair	79
	Folding stool, fifteenth century	79
	Reading desk, fifteenth century	80
	Chair, sixteenth century	81
85	Sculpture, on Italian chest	82
	Panel, English, fifteenth century	83
	„ German, fifteenth century	83
	„ French, sixteenth century	83
	„ Flemish, sixteenth century	83
90	Cabinet, French, 1600	84
	Table, French, 1600	85
	Cabinet, French, 1600	86
	Panel, English, 1590	87
	Venetian mirror frame	88
95	Chair, Dutch, 1690	89
	English table and chairs, 1633	92
	Ivory open work panel, 14th century	93
	Prehistoric carving on bone	95
	„ drawing upon slate	96
100	„ mammoth, upon ivory	96
	Leaf of Roman diptych	99
	Angel, in the British museum	100
	Cup, sixth century	101
	Side of early English casket	103
105	„ „ with inscription	103
	Two small panels in open work	104
	Cover of a box	105
	Comb, English, eleventh century	106
	„ Italian, sixteenth century	106
110	Mirror case	107
	Chessmen, twelfth century	107
	„ twelfth century	107
	Arm of a chair, twelfth century	108
	Head of pastoral staff, eleventh century	108
115	„ „ fourteenth century	109
	Pietà, in volute of a crozier	110
	Ivory painter at work	110
	Horn, fifteenth century	111
	Panel in open work	111
120	Leaf of diptych, English, 1350	112
	Indian comb	114

THE INDUSTRIAL ARTS.

		PAGE
	Chessmen found at Lewis	116
	Palissy dish	117
	Greek vase	121
125	Etruscan vase	125
	Samian ware, fragment	126
	„ bowl	127
	Gallic urn	128
	British bowl	128
130	Mediæval pottery	129
	Hispano-moresque vase	130
	Florentine terra-cotta	131
	Nevers bottle	132
	Rouen dish	132
135	„ vase	133
	Moustiers dish	134
	Palissy dish	134
	„ salt-cellar	135
	„ fruit plate	136
140	„ reptile dish	136
	„ cup, with shells	137
	„ dish	137
	„ mould	138
	Oiron ewer	139
145	„ candlestick	140
	„ vase and cup	141
	Sèvres vase	143
	Dresden candelabrum	145
	Delft vase	146
150	German ware, sixteenth century	147
	Mediæval English ewer	149
	Earthenware jug, French	150
	Wedgwood vase	152
	Oriental jar	154
155	Persian vase	156
	Chelsea vase	158
	Moustiers dish	160
	Maiolica plate	161
	Rhodian bowl	164
160	Persian wall tile	165
	Damascus plate	166
	Vase, with Arabic letters	167
	Valencia plateau	168
	Siculo-moresque bowl	169

THE INDUSTRIAL ARTS. xiii

		PAGE
165	Mezza-maiolica dish	170
	Luca della Robbia, medallion	171
	„ bas-relief	172
	Siena plate	173
	Pesaro dish	174
170	Faenza dish	175
	Urbino dish	176
	Gubbio bowl	176
	Plaque, by Giorgio	177
	Dish, by Giorgio	178
175	Castel Durante, plate	179
	Dish, with portrait of Perugino	180
	Dish, Xanto	181
	Bottle, Fontana	183
	Venetian dish	185
180	Vase, about 1500	186
	Cups, etc., German	187
	Enamelled oriental glass	194
	Stained glass	195
	„ Flemish	196
185	Venetian glass	198
	„ old enamelled	199
	„	200
	„ cups, etc.	201
	„ „	202
190	„ green, enamelled	202
	„ clear, ornamented	203
	„ cups, etc.	203
	„ cup, reticulated	204
	„ vases	204
195	„ mirror frame	205
	German glasses	206
	„ vases, etc.	207
	„ and Bohemian	208
	Window glass, English	210
200	Mosaic, ancient Roman; Kensington museum	211
	„ from battle of Issus	217
	„ antique Roman	218
	„ from Woodchester	219
	„ panel	220
205	„ from Avignon	221
	„ in Ara Cœli	223
	„ from Monreale	224

		PAGE
	Mosaic, Indian; from the Taj Mahal	226
	Mounted knight, fourteenth century	227
210	Barbarian soldier, in Roman service	230
	Norman archer	231
	Knights, from MS. of thirteenth century	232
	Mounted knight, twelfth century	233
	Helmet, thirteenth century	233
215	Suit of armour, fifteenth century	234
	Tournament helmet, fifteenth century	235
	Ancient cannon	235
	Arquebus, sixteenth century	236
	Moorish dagger	237
220	Knights in armour	238
	Ladies spinning and weaving, fifteenth century	239
	Indian woman reeling silk	243
	Vestments, twelfth century	247
	Silk damask, fifteenth century, Sicilian	250
225	" " Florentine	251
	The weaver, sixteenth century	252
	Orphrey of the Syon cope	253
	Tapestry, fourteenth century	254
	Hangings of a bed, fifteenth century	256
230	Guipure lace, seventeenth century	257
	Lace stitches	260
	Patterns of twisted threads	261
	Ancient point, Italian	262
	Raised Venetian point, seventeenth century	263
235	Guipure, seventeenth century	264
	Brussels lappet, eighteenth century	265
	Mechlin border, 1800	267
	Lappet, point d'Alençon	269
	Point d'Argentan	271
240	Honiton lace	274
	Irish point, modern	275
	Genoese point, sixteenth century	276

GOLD AND SILVER WORK.

Interior of a goldsmith's shop of the sixteenth century.

M. F. A.

GOLD AND SILVER WORK.

OLD is next to iron the most widely diffused metal on the face of the earth. It occurs in the primitive rocks, in the deposits derived from them, and in the vein-stones which traverse other geological formations. Gold is found only in the metallic state; sometimes crystallised, sometimes in threads of various sizes, sometimes in spangles or rounded grains.

From the very earliest ages after men multiplied, gathered themselves into communities and built cities, gold has been the representative of wealth and an external attribute of temporal dignity and power. We can easily supply the reasons why gold should have been so long and so universally valued. It was never plentiful, although to be found in so many districts of the world; for ages it was known to be the purest of metals; it does not rust or oxidize in the air nor does it tarnish by exposure; it is wonderfully ductile and malleable; and, lastly, the splendour and beauty of its colour are most attractive.

As to the ductility of gold, "of that spreading and oily metal" as an old writer calls it, we can point to the well-known gold leaf. The art of gold beating is of great antiquity, being referred to by Homer; and Pliny says that one ounce of gold could be extended to more than 600 leaves, each being four fingers square. In our own days the same quantity could be beaten into three times that number of leaves.

Silver also is found in many parts of the world, especially in Mexico and Peru. Few metals enter into a greater variety of natural combinations or are found over a wider geological range. It is said to exist in minute traces in some organic bodies and in the waters of the ocean. Like gold, it is exceedingly ductile and malleable; wire can be drawn from it finer than a human hair and when pure it is the brightest of all metals.

It is not possible to say at what date gold and silver, the two precious metals, were first worked into ornaments or used as coin or other circulating medium. In the Book of Genesis we read that Abraham when he went out of Egypt was very rich, not only in cattle but in silver and gold; and golden earrings and bracelets are spoken of in the twenty-fourth chapter. We believe that no coined gold or silver has been found in Egypt or in the ruins of Nineveh; and as a means of exchange it was probably at first used by weight.

But there is ample evidence of the very high antiquity of gold ornamental work. Many proofs may be seen in the paintings of Egyptian tombs, and (to name no more) there was a remarkable set of gold ornaments shown at the great Exhibition of 1862. These were found at Thebes in the tomb of a queen who reigned about 1500 years before the Christian æra. Among them was a poignard with a gold blade on which was engraved a combat between a lion and a bull: the cartouche contained the name of Amosis, son of the queen, and first king of the 18th dynasty. There were a diadem also, each extremity of which has a couching sphinx; and a square pectoral brooch, set with coloured stones; a massive bracelet, ornamented with a repoussé figure upon a ground of lapis lazuli; and a boat of massive gold upon four wheels of bronze, with silver rowers. Upon this last is the name of king Rameses, the father of Amosis. The most astonishing of the relics was a beautiful gold chain, of woven pattern and admirable workmanship, three feet long.

Almost coeval with these works in gold was the Exodus of the Jews from Egypt: and with such examples before us we cannot be surprised that the quantity "borrowed" by the Hebrews was so great and so rich that they were enabled to make from them the large number of sacred vessels concerning which we have detailed accounts in the Book of Exodus. Very probably the style of workmanship, although made according to a divine type and pattern, was like the wonderful jewels and gold ornaments of the Egyptian queen: and the workmen were chosen by Moses himself, who was learned in all the wisdom of the Egyptians. It is scarcely necessary to refer to the many places in the Scriptures where the gold and silver work of the tabernacle and the temple are described. The objects made in the desert were preserved until the building of Solomon's temple, when they were replaced by others of a richer and larger character. We know but little as to the shape and design of any of them, although some of the descriptions seem to be minute enough to give us a rough idea. The golden candlestick is a solitary exception, for a sculpture of it exists upon the arch of Titus, as it was when carried from Jerusalem to Rome.

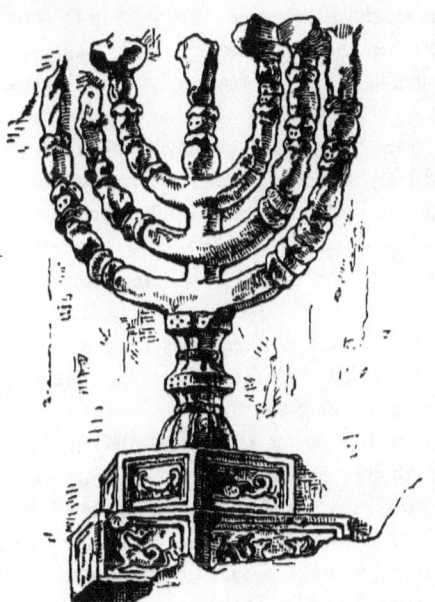

The golden candlestick, from the arch of Titus.

There were six branches, segments of circles curving out at regular intervals in three sets, which came to the same height above and ranged at one level with the centre light. The base was in two plinths, octagonal, and each panelled on the sides; with bas reliefs of winged animals. The lower part of the stem widens into a ring of conventional petals like an inverted lily. There is a well-known tradition that the candlestick itself was thrown into the Tiber when Maxentius fled in the fourth century. If there be any truth in this a future generation may yet see it, recovered from the bed of the river.

The Assyrians used gold largely for personal ornament and for decoration of buildings. Gilding was extensively employed, and some of the great statues may have been "overlaid with gold" like the cherubim in Solomon's temple. We must not forget, however, that a great authority (Mr. Layard) is inclined to believe that much of the metal called gold in the sacred scriptures and in profane authors of antiquity was in reality copper alloyed with other metals; like the famous bowls and plates discovered at Nineveh.

Passing from Egypt and oriental nations to the people of Greece and Italy we have far more to rely upon, both in examples still existing and in descriptions given by ancient writers. Presuming the age of Homer to be nearly a thousand years before Christ, even then the Greeks had spread into various countries along the shores of the Mediterranean, and colonies had been founded equal to the mother cities from whence they sprung. The colonists carried with them everywhere the precious metals and the art of working them.

We read in the poems of Homer and in other very early books that shields and armour and chariots were made of or decorated with gold: and a large quantity of gold and silver vessels and personal ornaments has been discovered within the last few years upon what is said to be the site of Troy and the palace of king Priam. Some centuries later, in the days of

Phidias and the great sculptors of that time, there is reason to believe that the goldsmith's art reached the highest degree of perfection. Not only were small works executed but colossal statues of mixed gold and ivory. All these have perished; although some remained perfect until long after Christianity had been accepted as the religion of the Roman empire. In fact, it is to the unhappy fanaticism of Christian zealots that we must attribute their destruction. With regard to smaller objects, vases, cups, and the like, it is not to be wondered at that in the lapse of so many centuries the intrinsic value of the materials was alone sufficient to tempt people, and barbarian conquerors especially, to break them up and melt them. Nevertheless, few as they are comparatively in number, we can learn from the specimens of ancient Greek gold and silver work which may be seen in most of the great national collections how excellent and elaborate was their workmanship.

We are indebted to the excavations which have been made in Etruria and especially in the tombs of that district for the finest examples now known of Greek work in gold. Of these it has been truly said by signor Castellani (whose judgment on the point is practical as well as sound) that we have obtained from the cemeteries of Etruria objects in gold of a workmanship so perfect that it is difficult to imitate or to explain the process of execution. He goes on to declare that he has never seen a single work in gold of after times, including even the most artistic periods, which can be compared for elegance of form or skill of handicraft with the archaic productions of Greek or Etruscan art. The Romans in imperial times undoubtedly had preserved certain primitive models, but their imitations in point of execution are extremely inferior.

The ancient ornaments buried in the tombs of Etruria are of two kinds; the one for use, the other for funeral purposes. The first are massive and might be worn for years without injury; the funeral ornaments are of extraordinary lightness and delicacy; in fact, too delicate to be worn. Both kinds, says signor Castellani, are generally in very pure gold; but in all cases the ancient process was quite different from that adopted in Europe in modern times. Modern goldsmith's work is less artistic and more mechanical. In examining an ancient Greek ornament our admiration of the materials, gold and precious stones, is far surpassed by that which is caused by the excellence of the workmanship. The most consummate skill and the best taste guided the hand of the artist whilst he was producing "repoussé" figures and decoration, or was disposing with perfect symmetry the small strings of minute granulated work.

The old Etruscan artists used mechanical agents which are now unknown to us, and were able to separate and join pieces of gold hardly perceptible to the naked eye. Modern workmen have failed in their attempts exactly to imitate the old ornaments. Nor do we know how the ancient processes of melting, soldering, and wire drawing were carried on. We are left therefore to admire, not alone the elegance and beauty of the Greek and Etruscan granulated and filigree works in gold, but the mode of execution also.

In the East Indies, at the present day, may be frequently seen wandering workers in gold and silver who carry their tools about with them, and where employment can be found soon transform coins and bits of the precious metal into filigree jewels or ornaments somewhat resembling the antique, whilst still following their own national and traditional style. These may give us some idea how the early Greeks and Etruscans worked.

Signor Castellani has taken great pains for many years in endeavouring to discover the primitive mode of working the delicate gold ornaments which have been discovered in the tombs. He says that the means of soldering was the first problem: and the almost invisible grains of gold, like fine sand, which give such a distinct character to Etruscan ornaments, presented nearly insurmountable difficulty. He read the treatises of mediæval goldsmiths, and the earlier books of Theophilus and Pliny; he enquired everywhere in Italy of all classes of jewellers; he made innumerable attempts, with all kinds of chemicals and the most powerful solvents, to compose the proper solder. At last he found some of the old processes still employed in a remote district, hidden in the recesses of the Apennines far from the great towns. Bringing away a few workmen he gave them much more instruction and at last succeeded, not perhaps in equalling but certainly in rivalling the brooches, chains, and other specimens of ancient Etruria and Greece.

It is not certain whether the old Egyptians were acquainted with the art of enamelling. Two late examples are known, but these are probably of the Ptolemaic age. No trace of enamel was on any of the beautiful objects which we have already mentioned, discovered in the tomb of the Pharaonic queen. The ornaments there set in the small divisions of the gold are little pieces of various stones. But, on the contrary, a considerable proportion of enamelled gold and silver ornaments of Greek and Etruscan work may be seen in many collections. These are not what may be called numerous; for the ancient artists seem to have employed enamel very sparingly; and to have been unwilling to hide gold which was extremely rare with a vitrified covering comparatively of little value. In fact, we cannot doubt that workmen who could so perfectly control the action of fire in soldering the finest atoms of gold, or who could twist gold wires of extreme fineness, or who could produce many varieties of enamel, could also, at their pleasure, cover the gold surface with enamel.

There are many Etruscan and Greek gold ornaments in national European collections: and among the most famous are the necklace in the British museum and some ear-rings found at Vulci.

In the time of the Roman empire there must have been large accumulations at Rome of works in the precious metals: but from causes which any one can easily suggest, war, plunder, the necessities of poverty and the like, very few indeed have come down to our own day. These, with scarcely an exception, have been discovered buried in the ground. There are allusions and references without end in almost every classic author to objects of this kind, as being eagerly sought after by the wealthy and luxurious: and we find not only the works mentioned but the names of some of the best artists. Two fine examples of Greek vessels in gold may be seen in the British museum: one is the outer shell or ornamental part of a drinking cup, embossed; the other a *patera* or saucer found in Sicily, having four balls in relief in the inside.

Among the most important specimens of Roman work in silver are the cups and other vessels which form what is called "the Treasure of Hildesheim." This consists of thirty pieces of silver; cups, vases, dishes, a tray,

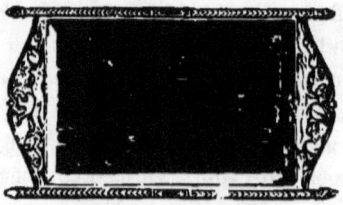

Silver tray from Hildesheim.

parts of candelabra, and other furniture of a dining table, many of them of beautiful design and workmanship, embossed and in some instances parcel gilt. They were found in 1868 by Prussian soldiers who were digging a trench for some military practice; and at first their great value was not recognised. Further examination proved how important the discovery was, and the whole collection is now preserved in the museum at Berlin. The pieces do not appear to be all of the same date; the best of them perhaps as early as the first century, and others as late probably as the second. Various speculations have been advanced as to their original ownership; it is quite certain that they are the work of some of the chief artists in gold and silver of the day, but it is not easy to account for their having been carried to a distance so far from Rome. They may have been (perhaps five or six centuries after they were made) part of the treasure of some great religious house to which they had been given, and have been concealed during an outbreak or barbarian invasion in the troubled times before Charlemagne. Or they might have been part of the travelling baggage of some wealthy Roman sent on a mission into Germany, or of the camp equipage of a general in command of troops, from either of whom they might have been plundered and then concealed and the record about them lost or in time forgotten. The largest piece is a vase of oval shape with small handles, and of a form common in the old terra cotta vases of the Greeks. It is enriched with delicate arabesque work of leaves, scrolls, cupids and sphinxes in relief. Another is a bowl or cup with concave sides relieved by

Outside of a bowl or cup from Hildesheim.

Interior of same cup.

a beautiful fringe of Greek flower ornament; half of the inside of the cup is filled with a seated figure of Minerva draped and helmeted, and leaning on a shield. The woodcuts show the inside and outside of this bowl. All the pieces have been reproduced in electrotype, exact copies, by Messrs. Christoffle of Paris: and a set is in the South Kensington museum.

Another remarkable collection of Roman silver work is in the British museum; of much later date, and of a style and manner of execution which prove how greatly the arts had declined. These are probably of the sixth century, and consist of the different articles of the toilet of a lady. They were found enclosed in a large coffer or box, also of silver and decorated with repoussé work: the coffer is preserved with them.

A few small silver vases or cruets, perhaps of the fourth century, are in the museum of the Vatican; these, though made for use in Christian worship bear a great resemblance to the cups which may be seen in ancient representations of pagan sacrifices for libations; nor is it surprising that the Christian goldsmiths were content to imitate old types and patterns, having as yet no peculiar style of their own.

Our space will not permit the enumeration of even the very few examples, which still exist in museums, of gold and silver work of the first ten centuries of our æra. The most important are the gifts of queen Theodolinda, early in the seventh century, to the cathedral church of Monza, where they yet remain. Besides these are a richly decorated box enclosing an Evangelisterium (selections from the Gospels), and the famous "iron crown" of the kings of Italy. The crown is so called from the circlet of iron incrusted in the interior, said to have been forged out of one of the nails which fastened our Saviour to the cross. The crown itself is a kind of jointed collar in gold, rather less than three inches wide, loaded with uncut sapphires, emeralds, and rubies interspersed with flowers of gold. Apart from its intrinsic interest and antiquity it possesses but little merit, and again shows how degenerate was the artistic talent of the Lombard goldsmith of the sixth century.

GOLD AND SILVER WORK.

A votive crown of a king of the Visigoths, about the year

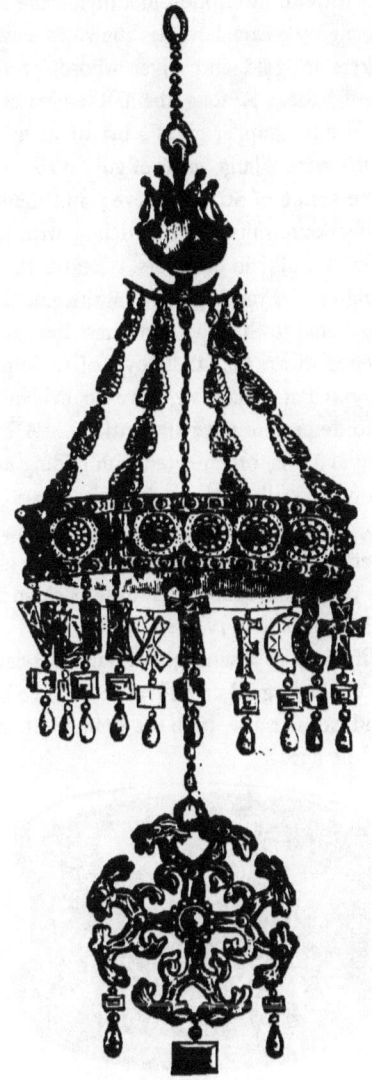

Votive crown of king Suintila.

630, is preserved at Madrid: it is of massive gold, with sapphires and pearls; and with an inscription identifying the king, Suintila.

France, some eighty years later, is known to have had among her artists workers in gold and silver whose productions were renowned far and wide. Among them, the greatest was Eligius or saint Eloy. His biographer gives a list of many of his works, the chief of which were a large cross of gold made for the basilica of St. Denis.; the shrine of St. Geneviève; and the shrine of gold "of surpassing workmanship" and enriched with jewels, to contain the relics of St. Martin of Tours. Before the revolution of 1790 many churches in France gloried in the possession of goldsmith's work, attributed to St. Eloy: but these have been destroyed or stolen and melted down (like the crown of Agilulph stolen from the public library at Paris) and we have no evidence which will now enable us to determine their authenticity. A bronze seat in the public library at Paris, ornamented with gilding and engraving, has been traditionally said for many hundred years to have been made by St. Eloy for his patron, king Dagobert; modern criticism is disposed rather to think that the lower part only is ancient, probably before the reign of Dagobert, and the back and arms to have been added in the tenth century.

We have no difficulty in asserting that, rare as existing examples are, numberless works in gold and silver must have been made for ecclesiastical and secular use from the time of St. Eloy onwards through the middle ages.

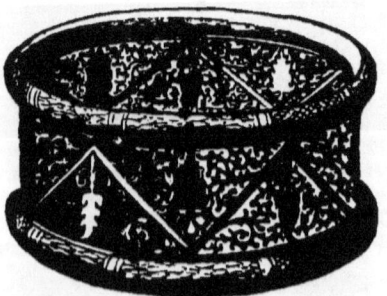

Gaulish armlet, gold: in public library at Paris.

GOLD AND SILVER WORK.

There is scarcely any historical record of those centuries which does not supply us with evidence of this fact. We can have no doubt that Charlemagne gave encouragement to Byzantine goldsmiths and jewellers as he did to artists in ivory and enamel and mosaic: princes and bishops rivalled each other in the magnificence of the gifts offered to the churches and monasteries restored by his order. Charlemagne's will is a curious evidence also of the riches of gold and silver work which he himself possessed. Among other objects he had three tables of silver and one of gold. On the first was traced the plan, on another a view, of the city of Rome: a third was composed of three zones, containing a description of the whole universe. When he was buried he was enclosed in a chamber under the church of Aix-la-

The crown of Charlemagne.

Chapelle, seated upon a throne in his imperial robes: by his side a sword decorated with gold on the pommel and the scabbard: and before him were suspended his sceptre and shield, also of gold. The crown and sword have been preserved to our own days, and are kept in the imperial treasury at Vienna. The crown is composed of eight plates of gold, four larger than the others, connected by hinges. The large plates are studded with precious stones, the smaller are enamelled. There are Latin inscriptions but the whole seems to be of Byzantine workmanship. The full length of the scabbard of the sword is overlaid with gold, and enriched with cloisonné enamels.

A number of small objects, rings and brooches, or portions of crosses and crucifixes, may be seen in many collections; the works of goldsmiths and silversmiths in England, France, Germany and Italy from the ninth to the fifteenth century. Of larger pieces we must mention the golden "table" or altar front

The golden altar front from Basle.

given by the emperor Henry the second (whose golden crown and that of his empress are in the treasury of the king of Bavaria) about the year 1020, to the cathedral of Basle. This is now in the museum of the hôtel Cluny. It is nearly six feet wide, in form a Romanesque arcade of five arches under which stands our Lord (in the centre) with three archangels and St. Benedict. The whole is executed in repoussé work in high relief. Again, the celebrated Pala d'Oro or golden frontal of the church of St. Mark at Venice; the finest specimen of enamelled gold which has been handed down to us of the work of the eleventh century: this is unquestionably of Byzantine execution, having been ordered to be made at Constantinople and brought from thence. Again, the golden altar of St. Ambrose at Milan, of the ninth century, decorated with enamels; the front being entirely of gold, the sides and back of silver enriched with gold. Again, in the public library at Paris is a service book written about 850 for Charles the bald with ivory covers enclosed in silver filigree work adorned with precious stones; and in the British museum is a silver reliquary, in the form of a head, of the eleventh century, purchased a few years ago from the cathedral of Basle.

Most of these and other similar but less important pieces have a distinct Byzantine character; and in those cases in which we have external evidence of their origin we see that the Greeks preserved, down to the twelfth century, their pre-eminence in art over other nations.

During the succeeding centuries, as civilisation spread over Europe, the desire to possess rich vessels and ornaments made of the precious metals naturally increased. Not only kings and princes encouraged artists everywhere but religious houses ordered splendid works for the use of their churches, and the laity offered innumerable gifts. The great guilds of the chief cities of England and France supplied themselves also with cups and salvers and all kinds of furniture for their tables. Although by far the greater

GOLD AND SILVER WORK.

part of these productions has been destroyed in the lapse of so many generations (and more especially in England the eccle-

Shrine, copper gilt; twelfth century.

siastical gold and silver work at the period of the reformation) we not only have ample, and in some cases detailed, accounts of the more valuable pieces in mediæval histories and documents, especially in inventories and wills, but enough examples are still extant to enable us to judge sufficiently both the artistic quality of the design and the excellence of execution.

Our space enables us to offer only a very brief notice of a few of these, which may be found in England. Among the regalia in the Tower is kept the coronation spoon,

The Coronation spoon.

used at the anointing; the date of this is early in the thirteenth century. We engrave also the "ampulla" or "dove," which is used also at the same ceremony: for although work of about the year 1660, it probably is a reproduction of the earlier and destroyed

The coronation "ampulla"; gold.

piece. The "Lynn cup" belongs to the corporation of that town, and is wrongly said by old tradition to have been given by king John. But it is not earlier than about 1350, as is clear from the costume of the figures enamelled upon it. It is a tall standing cup and cover in silver gilt, and the enamels are translucent; the slender stem springs from a shallow circular foot, edged below with a flat pentagonal base. The knob of the stem has five acorn-shaped projections. This beautiful cup has been repaired more than once; nevertheless it is one of the most remarkable specimens existing in this country of the work of the period to which it belongs.

Of about the same date is a silver gilt cover, decorated with cloisonné and champlevé enamels, preserved at All Souls college, Oxford; where are also a crystal salt, of the end of the century, with silver gilt mounts; and a mazer bowl probably given to the college by the founder, archbishop Chichele, about 1440.

Many of these "mazers" are in English collections, generally mounted with a silver rim and occasionally lined with silver, sometimes of rich and good workmanship. The name is probably derived from the old name for the maple tree, *masaru* or *masere;* but although, strictly, none but a maple-wood vessel is a mazer, the wood employed was not always of maple. In a still more loose way of speaking, silver cups made in the common shape of mazers are sometimes so called. A very early example exists at Harbledown hospital, Canterbury; of the time of Edward the first: and another at Saffron Walden, with an engraved representation of the Virgin and Child inside the bowl. Mazer cups have in some instances inscriptions. On one in the vestry of York minster is engraved a grant of so many days "pardon." On another, in private hands, is

"In the name of the Trinite,
Fille the kup and drink to me."

At Oxford are also the pastoral staffs of bishop Fox, English work of the fifteenth century; and of William of Wykeham who died in 1404. This last is a most important and elaborate specimen of silversmith's work of the fourteenth century. The staff itself is wood, overlaid with silver, gilt and enamelled. The head is of Gothic architectural design, octagonal, and decorated with a series of statuettes of saints under canopies. The curve of the staff is richly crocketed, and has on both sides a series of translucent enamels representing angels playing on musical instruments. The curve below is maintained by a winged angel resting on a bracket formed of a bearded head. At Queen's college is a drinking horn with a silver gilt band or mounting, English, about the year 1380.

At Cambridge are two fine cups with covers; one of the fifteenth century, the other, as shown by the hall mark, made in 1507. These are at Christ's college. At Corpus Christi college is a very early drinking-horn, with silver gilt mounting, given in 1352. The mounts consist of a scalloped band nearly an inch deep round the lip, and a battlemented band round the centre resting on strap-shaped supports to sustain the horn. A terminal ornament composed of a crowned head rises from an openwork turret.

GOLD AND SILVER WORK.

In the Tower is preserved a small and light sceptre, ivory mounted in gold and enamelled; and said to have been made for the coronation of Anne Boleyn.

It is impossible for us in so limited a space to name any more examples; and as regards plate and gold and silver ornaments of the sixteenth century, beautiful relics are so numerous that a description of them is sure to be found in the catalogue of almost any collection. The most important ever brought together were probably the famous "Loan collection" at South Kensington, in 1862, and another at Ironmongers'.Hall in 1861.

The largest proportion of gold and silver work which now exists, made in the mediæval times, was originally for sacred use and for church decoration. This is so, in spite of the terrible destruction of all such works of art, however beautiful, in England about the year 1550, and in France during the first revolution. Naturally, we might expect it: because reverence was always shown during the middle ages to the possessions of churches and monasteries and they escaped being plundered; nor, again, could communities easily dispose of them to meet any temporary occasion or necessity. And another reason; in many instances not a few of the shrines and reliquaries and other ornaments of churches were themselves held sacred and to be carefully preserved.

On the other hand, we must not too hastily attribute the loss of innumerable specimens of ancient and mediæval work in the precious metals to great national changes and troubles, like the two just alluded to. Many causes, always prevalent, constantly led to the destruction of objects intrinsically so valuable. A very powerful agent must also be recognised in the universal and never ceasing desire for novelty. Scarcely an ornament of one generation seems to have found favour in the eyes of its successor. Times change, and with them customs and manners

The sceptre (so called) of Anne Boleyn.

and fashion: and goldsmiths and jewellers were doubtless always engaged in breaking up, to pay for the new fancies of the son, the very works on which their predecessors had laboured to please the father.

Chalices still exist which can be attributed to any period since the year 1200; and their varying style and decoration supply a good deal of information as to the art and workmanship of the different periods and countries where they were made. We give woodcuts of eight chalices, in the South Kensington museum, of

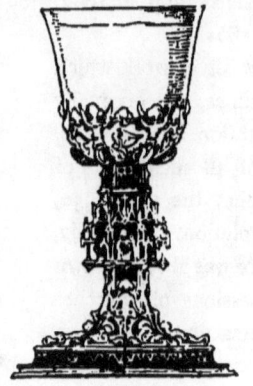

German; about 1450 (no. 631. '65).

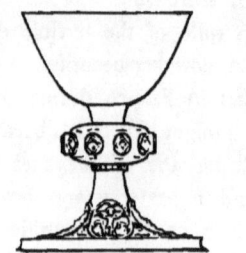

French, 14th century (no. 4903. '59)

German, about 1520 (no. 6971. '61).

Spanish, 1549 (no. 132. '73).

GOLD AND SILVER WORK.

Italian, 14th cent.? (no. 237. '74).

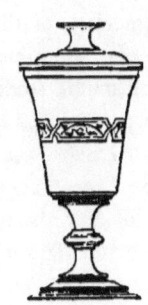

English, with pa en; about 1550 (no. 4636. '58).

German, 15th century (no. 2102. '55).

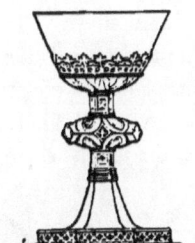

German, 14th century (no. 236. '74).

the workmanship of different countries. The first, no. 631'68 is remarkably rich; and was bought for £800. In very early ages chalices were of large size; but few examples of these, if any, can be referred to: after the eleventh century they became comparatively small. The bowl is invariably perfectly plain inside and also for some distance outside below the lip. The ornamental decoration was applied, in enamels or embossed work, to the foot and stem. Some chalices of the fifteenth and sixteenth centuries are elaborately enriched; the cup itself is covered with enamels, the knob with figures in full relief, and the foot with pierced or open work. The simplicity and severity of the old style and canonical rules gradually gave way as time passed on. We might speak of shrines and reliquaries and crosses, of mitres or brooches (morses), of thuribles, of candlesticks and book covers, as of chalices; they are the best authorities to which we can refer for goldsmiths' work of the middle ages.

The most precious shrine of mediæval workmanship now existing is perhaps that in the cathedral of Orvieto, which contains the "corporale di Bolsena." This was executed in the year 1338 by an artist of Siena; it is of silver and weighs 4 cwt. It represents the façade of the cathedral, and is decorated with panels of translucent enamel, giving a history of the well-known "miracle of Bolsena."

From the year 1250 for three hundred years we have in various records the names of many great workers and artists in gold and silver. The political division of Italy into petty sovereignties and the liberty enjoyed in some of the great municipalities were eminently favourable to the development of luxury of all kinds. The armour of the great nobility, their plate, the jewels of ladies,

Scent box, in chased gold; French, 16th century.

the furniture for churches and altars, all supplied incessant occupation for goldsmiths; and some of the most renowned sculptors

GOLD AND SILVER WORK.

of those centuries, Ghiberti, Brunelleschi, and Donatello are said to have first practised and learnt their art from goldsmiths. The art of working in niello, which consists in covering with a kind of black enamel fine engraving upon silver was, at the same period, a branch of goldsmith's work. The most famous of such artists was Maso Finiguerra, who lived about 1450. No one ever equalled him in engraving so many figures on so small a space and with such excellent correctness of drawing. Among the nielli on silver preserved at Florence is a pax by Finiguerra; and this is the more interesting as being the plate from which the first engraving of the kind was ever printed, and of which the only extant impression is in the public library at Paris. So that the fame of Finiguerra rests not only on his

Pendant of the goldsmiths of Ghent, 15th century.

GOLD AND SILVER WORK.

merit as a goldsmith but as the inventor of taking impressions from engravings upon metal.

We can mention, here, only one other name; and that, probably the best known of all; Benvenuto Cellini. He was born in 1500, and having spent some years as an apprentice in one or two

Pendant, attributed to Cellini; in the public library at Paris.

of the best workshops of Florence he worked in several towns of Italy. As time passed he established the highest reputation, and was largely employed at Rome by pope Clement the seventh. Unfortunately Cellini was ordered by that pope to destroy as well as to make; and to his hand we must trace the destruction of numberless artistic treasures which probably might, or at least some among them, have come down to our own days. Whilst Clement was besieged in the castle of St. Angelo, Cellini tells us in his memoirs that he received orders to unset all the precious stones that were upon the tiaras, the sacred vessels, and vestments of the pope, and to melt down the gold; of which he obtained two hundred weight. We need not wonder, judging from this instance alone, why it is that so very few pieces of ancient and mediæval gold and silver work can now be found. Afterwards Cellini went to France and was patronised by Francis the first: yet, though he executed there many splendid works, only one can be identified; a gold salt-cellar, preserved in the museum at Vienna.

Besides this salt-cellar probably only one or two medals and two cups (one crystal, the other lapis-lazuli, mounted in enamelled gold) kept in the gallery at Florence can be absolutely authenticated as Cellini's work; yet he must have made, during fifty years of life, a very large number of pieces in gold and silver. All cannot have perished, and whilst we should be very cautious before we hastily set down, as many will, any very fine renaissance cup or jewel as Cellini's work, yet it is not unreasonable to attribute to him some of the best examples in great collections both at home and abroad. But these ought all to be carefully compared, as far as may be, with his really known pieces, and with the account which he has himself given in his published treatise of the artistic processes which he employed.

Cellini was not the only great goldsmith of his time. Then, and in the early part of the seventeenth century, there were

GOLD AND SILVER WORK.

Lapis-lazuli, with gold mount. Italian; 16th century.

Rock crystal, silver gilt mount. Italian; 16th century.

very eminent artists not only in Italy but in France and England whose works are scarcely if at all inferior to his. To mention English work; we have specimens in the Kensington museum and in many private collections, chalices, cups, dishes, and smaller objects of the highest quality both in design and execution. The woodcuts represent several examples.

English sugar-sifter; about 1580 (no. 551. '74).

Basin; English; 1684 (no. 469. '64).

GOLD AND SILVER WORK.

Augsburg: about 1600 (no. 7941. '62).

English; 1611 (no. 5964. '59).

English; 1650 (no. 36. '65).

Cup and cover; English; 1660 (no. 7242. '61).

GOLD AND SILVER WORK.

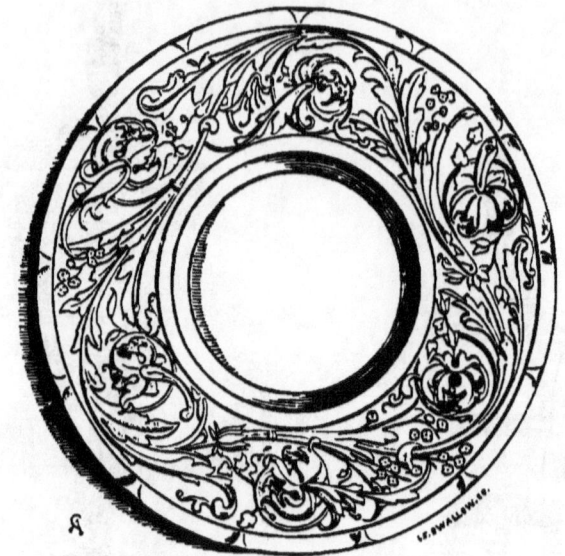

Flemish; about 1670 (no. 1153. '53).

Nuremberg; about 1650 (no. 3637. '56)

So also in Germany; Nuremberg and Augsburg were especially famous; and in the later years of the sixteenth century, the German goldsmiths dropped so much of the earlier national feeling and adopted so largely the Italian style and manner that it is not easy always to distinguish whose the work may be. A fair guide is the form of the cups or vases; which always retained a certain stamp of originality. Moreover, nothing can be more graceful than the arabesques which enrich German work of that date in the precious metals, or more exquisite than the twisted figures which supply the handles.

We give also some woodcuts of English plate of the last century.

Repoussé work, which has been more than once spoken of, is the art of beating up silver, gold, or other metals: in ordinary practice, an alternation of pressing out from the back and of beating in from the face. A plate (say) of silver of about the thickness of a shilling is fixed on an elastic cement. The outline of the design being traced with a punch, the forms are beaten into relief with a hammer, whilst the cement beneath prevents the rending of the metal. When the required relief is obtained the

English; about 1710 (no. 943. '09).

Tureen at Windsor castle, 1773.

Kettle, at Windsor castle, 1732.

English; 1770 (no. 564, '74).

Silver table, at Windsor castle: about 1700.

plate is turned over on the same cement, and the forms corrected by beating back and perfected by means of chasing.

Before we end, it will be right to make a few brief observations upon English hall-marks. These enable us to ascribe any piece of plate, so marked, to the exact year in which it may have been made. The necessity of adding a certain amount of alloy with gold and silver, which in the perfectly pure state are too soft and ductile, has called for the employment of a standard of fine quality by which the real value of the worked material might be known. The privilege of assaying precious metals was conferred upon the Goldsmiths' Company as far back as the year 1300 by a statute which declared also the required quality of the metal which should be used. Within sixty or seventy years afterwards we find that three distinct marks were to be impressed on every piece which was examined: namely, the assay mark, probably a letter of the alphabet; the initials of the maker; and the leopard's head crowned. Later statutes have made various regulations, all directed to prevent deception by dishonest makers and inflicting penalties on transgressors. The stamps at present impressed in London on all plate at Goldsmiths' hall are, for silver, the leopard's head; the lion passant; the date mark, a letter of the alphabet; the maker's mark; and the queen's head: for gold, a crown and 22 or 18 according to standard.

Other towns besides London have assay offices with some token of distinction; such as Chester, Dublin, and Edinburgh, etc.

Very fine examples of Elizabethan and earlier English plate which have not been marked are in many collections. The omission is always unfortunate; not so much because a doubt may occasionally arise as to whether the piece may or may not be of English work, but because we have no other absolutely certain guide to the exact date. The first date which is now known upon any piece of plate is 1445; which is to be found upon a grace-cup (ivory mounted in silver gilt) in the possession of Mr. Howard, of Corby; and upon a silver spoon said to have belonged to Henry the sixth, preserved at Hornby castle in Lancashire. After that year there are many blank years; of which no extant pieces have been discovered; we have 1481, 1487, 1497, and 1499: from the beginning of the sixteenth century, and especially since 1520, a tolerably complete series can be referred to.

The English silver standard, or sterling, which term first occurs in the reign of Henry the second, was of the fineness of 11 oz. 2 dwts. in the pound troy, and 18 dwts. of alloy. This has continued with an interruption of about twenty years in the sixteenth century to the present time. In computing the standard of gold, the word "carat" is employed; the carat being the 24th part of a pound or an ounce troy. There are two standards for gold, as for silver: for gold, 22 and 18 carats of pure metal in every ounce, the ounce containing 24 carats. The coinage of England is of the higher standard; the lower is used for manufacturing purposes, except for wedding rings. The standards for silver are 11 oz. 10 dwts. and 11 oz. 2 dwts. in every pound. The higher standard is scarcely ever used; not even for our coins.

Hall marks are not limited to Great Britain and Ireland. They are ordered in France and Austria and other foreign states; under statutes and decrees enforcing penalties as in our own country. Among these foreign marks the pine-apple of Augsburg, the N of Nuremberg, and the imperial eagle of Austria are probably the best known. Very useful lists of these continental marks may be referred to in the South Kensington "Art library."

Pendant, with diamonds; seventeenth century.

BRONZE, COPPER, AND IRON.

Censer; twelfth century.

M. F. A.

BRONZE, COPPER, AND IRON.

WE must speak, in this section, more briefly than of gold and silver, of works in iron, copper, and bronze: this last is a compound of copper, tin, and other alloys.

Although our subject is chiefly concerned with the execution of small objects in metal, it may not be improper to remark that the general employment of iron in modern days for the purposes of construction in buildings is owing to its strength, elasticity, toughness, and durability, qualities which obviate many difficulties otherwise insuperable. On the other hand great care is required in order to avoid the violation of the laws of good taste and proportion. Architects cannot but use iron largely in many buildings; but no ornament peculiarly identified with stone or marble should be introduced, nor any construction in iron which could be better executed in another material. A needless display of strength is as objectionable as weakness; and iron-work should never be obtrusive.

The sacred writings contain many references to the very early employment of various metals for domestic use and personal ornaments. We read in the Pentateuch of the riches of Abraham, of the jewellery offered to Rebecca, of the cup given by Joseph to his brother: of molten and graven images, of iron tools, beaten work, brazen vessels, and the like. The ancient Egyptians were skilled workers in metal, and so also were the Assyrians.

Classical writers, Greek and Latin, are full of references to and descriptions of numerous works in metal. Armour and weapons it need scarcely be said, were amongst the most frequent objects and naturally would advance in merit and beauty of workmanship from the plain spear head, hatchet, or shield of primitive ages to the period of the best Greek art. The Egyptians and the Greeks had some means of hardening and tempering their instruments of bronze, with which we are unacquainted. No example as a work of art is to be found in any collection more exquisite than two portions of the fittings of a breastplate or cuirass in the British museum. These fragments represent two groups in very high relief, the subject of each being a combat between a Greek warrior and an Amazon. In both groups the Amazon has fallen on one knee; the antagonist kneels against her side, grasping her hair with one hand. The relief is so prominent that some of the most salient parts, the hands, the knees, and some part of the draperies, appear almost to be detached from the ground. In the heads the plate is reduced to the thickness of a sheet of writing paper, and on the reverse are cavities nearly an inch deep. These fragments have been long and deservedly celebrated as the finest existing examples of such work. They were found in 1820, in Lucania, in southern Italy. In 1833 they were purchased for £1000 for the British museum by a subscription, to which the trustees contributed £200. The size of each fragment is about six by seven inches.

Bronze is an alloy much harder than copper, and was employed before the method of working iron was understood; and has the important property of attaining various degrees of hardness according to the rate of cooling from the fused state. When rapidly cooled it is soft; when slowly, hard. Thus tools of bronze could be made capable of fashioning the same metal in a softer condition. The Phœnicians in very early times, perhaps a thousand years before the Christian æra, traded largely with England, and taking home the mineral ores from Cornwall and Devon probably supplied the eastern nations with the necessary materials. A systematic analysis of the bronze weapons and works of art of all periods which are still extant, found in different localities, would doubtless throw great light upon this important branch of ancient and mediæval industry.

The term bronze has been generally adopted by archæologists to designate a mixed metal composed chiefly of copper with an alloy of tin, which latter is generally found to range from eight to ten per cent. Copper ores are more or less abundantly distributed in almost every country of the world. Cyprus seems to have been one of the earliest sources of this metal used by the ancients; but the mines of Spain, Anglesea, and Cornwall were also known to them. We have abundant proof that the Romans worked copper mines in England and Wales; their tools and stamped cakes of the metal having been found. Picks, bronze celts, and wooden shovels of Roman and even earlier times, have been discovered in the stream tin workings of Cornwall. By the melting together of these two ores, copper and tin, bronze is produced, differing in colour from either of the constituent elements as also in other qualities. In place of metals, the one white, the other ruby colour, we obtain a closer substance of a golden brown.

In Britain and in Ireland celts or axes, swords and other weapons, were made in great quantities in extremely remote and even prehistoric times. Many of the examples which have been discovered in excavations and in old burial places are of good workmanship and design. The collections of the British museum and of the Royal Irish Academy possess some admirable specimens. A few of the moulds from which the objects were cast have also been found. Before the art of casting was discovered statues were formed of hammered plates, fastened together by rivets. An intermediate improvement was introduced (it is said) at Chios, by which the pieces were soldered instead of being riveted. The earliest cast pieces were solid.

It may be well here to give, as briefly as possible, a description of the usual process adopted for casting in bronze. When lightness is requisite, and economy in the use of metal, statues and other objects are not made solid but are cast over a central core. This is first built up to a rude outline, of a material composed generally of modelling clay mixed with pounded brick and plaster of Paris. When fashioned it is carefully dried, and the last moisture driven out by baking in an oven. Upon this core, which in the case of a large statue is further supported by iron bars, modelling wax is overlaid of the required thickness. Upon this wax the sculptor works; and the statue leaves his hands in wax, to be replaced by bronze. Outside this the mould is formed; and the greatest care is necessary that every minute detail shall be filled in with the composition and without the slightest disturbance or abrasion of the finished waxen surface. The mould is usually a mixture of dried clay and pounded crucibles with some plaster of Paris and ground down with water to the consistence of cream. Layer upon layer, thickening as each gradually dries, is cautiously placed upon the mould, and so that no air is left in bubbles: afterwards upon the outside is formed a stouter coating of coarser quality to sustain the inner mould and to bear the weight of metal. Thus prepared, after slow drying, the whole is firmly fixed within an oven, and the mass is heated until the wax within has flowed out in a liquid state from every corner. The core and mould are kept in their proper positions by means of small rods of bronze, which had been previously inserted in the core, passing through the wax, and with the other ends embedded in the mould. The liquid metal is then tapped from the furnace and poured steadily into the mould, filling every line and detail which the wax had occupied. After cooling, the mould is carefully broken away, the core raked out, and all superfluous metal, the connecting-rods, and other rough parts removed. Then the statue is complete, not as the artist left it in wax but in enduring bronze.

The use of bronze in sculpture is of very high antiquity. An Egyptian figure in that material is mentioned by Sir Gardner Wilkinson with an inscription containing a date more than 2000 years before Christ. We do not know when casting in bronze was first introduced into Greece; but some idea of the extent of its employment soon after the time of Alexander the great may be formed from the record, that the Roman consul in the year 130 B.C. found at Athens three thousand bronze statues, and as many at Rhodes and at Olympia. Of the countless statues which must have been executed during the flourishing age of Athens, and of the Roman empire, comparatively very few have been preserved to our own time; the value of the bronze led to their destruction. Of large works the horses at Venice, the colossal figure of Hercules now in the Vatican, the equestrian statue of Marcus Aurelius, with a few others of life-size, are almost the only examples which remain. Antique bronzes of smaller size are to be found in most museums, in the Louvre, in the British museum, and especially at Naples from Pompeii and Herculaneum. Many of these are admirable as works of sculpture and for the excellence of their technical qualities.

In no country was the early production of bronze implements brought to greater perfection than in our own: and we may perhaps even go further and say that, both with regard to the beauty of form and perfection of casting, the old inhabitants of Britain rivalled the manipulative skill of good workmen of the present day. This is equally true of the workmanship of the shields and other objects, in the later Celtic period, which were not only sometimes enriched with enamel, but as carefully executed in relief, like many of the more developed productions of Etruria. We must further bear in mind that these were the work, for the most part, of a people who knew not and were independent of Roman civilization.

We dare not venture upon the chronology of the bronze period: it must have varied in its development from different centres. The variety and number of the instruments and weapons of that time which have been discovered are very great. We have celts or axes, often ornamented by punching and hammering, or with patterns in relief; spears and arrow-heads; sickles, files, and the like; personal ornaments, such as torques or collars, armlets, rings, and buttons. The British museum is rich in collections of these objects.

Antique bronzes which have been long buried in the ground acquire a kind of green rust, or *patina*, which is one great proof of genuineness. This *patina* varies with the nature of the soil; and in some cases the surface acquires the smoothness and colour of malachite. It is extremely difficult to imitate the natural *patina*, but so important is it as an evidence of authenticity that numerous attempts have been made in order to pass off forgeries of the antique.

We have in early records soon after the reign of Constantine many notices of gifts to churches of works in bronze, showing that casting and chasing in that material were still carried on. The most important work which has been preserved from those days to our own is the seated statue of St. Peter in that saint's basilica at Rome, a work ordered by Leo the first, about the year 450. Its general aspect is that of a senatorial figure, and unusually good for the debased art of that period: not wanting in a certain rigid dignity, and remarkable for a technical skill and finish, which would support the opinion that it may be the work of a Byzantine artist. The chair or throne of Dagobert, now in the Louvre, is another famous bronze ascribed to the seventh century.

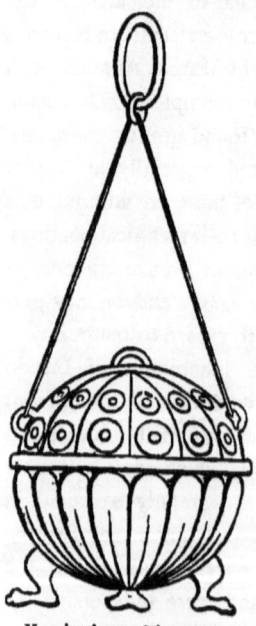

Hanging lamp; 9th century; from a contemporary MS.

But, speaking generally, it would seem that Italy about the tenth century had nearly lost the art of casting in bronze, and of working in bas-relief. The gates ordered for the church of St. Paul at Rome were made at Constantinople, where the ancient method of working had still been preserved by tradition. Some bronze works executed about that time in Germany for the cathedral at Augsburg and for the tomb of Rodolph at Merseburg bear also a certain stamp of Byzantine character, as if workmen had been brought from Constantinople to melt and chase the metal.

Admirable works in copper executed in Ireland about the eleventh century are still preserved. We engrave the so-called St. Patrick's bell, cleverly inlaid with gold filigree and set with crystals.

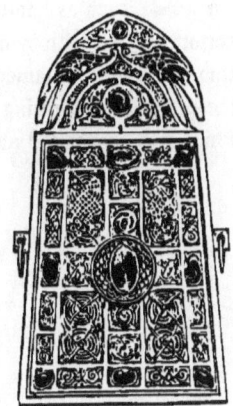

The bell of St. Patrick.

Very beautiful things were made in western Europe for ecclesiastical

Bell; of the twelfth century.

purposes; such as handbells, of which the woodcut is an example, perforated and with symbols representing the four evangelists. A common sacred ornament of churches about the same period was the dove for preserving the pyx with the blessed Sacrament, and which was suspended above the altar. These are now excessively

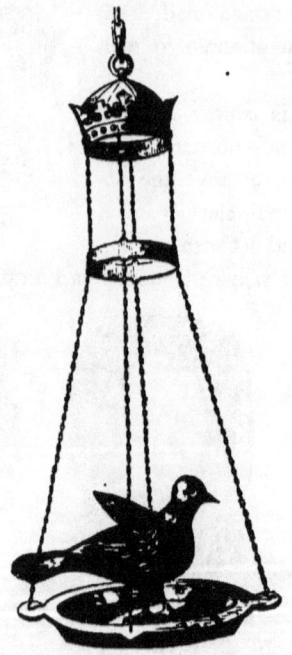

Dove; thirteenth century.

rare; and are to be seen only in a few collections. The use of them dropt out before the fifteenth century, and when no longer required they were probably broken up. Episcopal croziers are preserved in many museums: these, as were also the doves, shrines, handbells, etc., were generally enamelled. As time went on, numberless objects were produced for ornament in private

Crozier or bishop's staff; thirteenth century.

houses, for personal use, or for decoration of churches. Our space permits no more than the mere mention of these: the first woodcut on the next page represents a curious specimen in the Kensington museum, no. 245, '74.

About the beginning of the thirteenth century the process of casting bronze had reappeared in Italy, and was soon successfully practised there. Then, and in the next centuries, very famous works were executed, still existing. In Rome, in the Lateran baptistery, is a small pair of solid cast doors, of the date of 1195, with a few figures in relief and other designs in incised lines. A

BRONZE AND IRON.

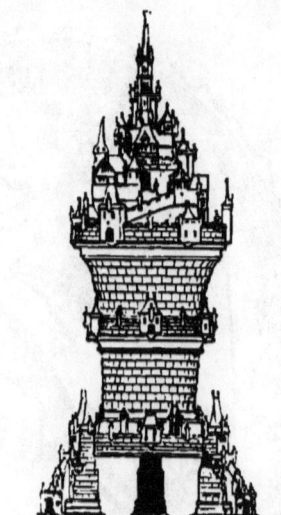

Gilt metal; German; sixteenth century.

Candlestick; Italian; sixteenth century.

wonderful candlestick, of the same period, is preserved in the cathedral at Milan. The gates of the Duomo at Pisa and of San Martino at Lucca, of the baptistery at Florence and many others, testify to the rapid progress in perfection and beauty of workmanship. The great artists were Nicola Pisano and his son Giovanni, Brunelleschi, Ghiberti, and Donatello. Smaller objects of equal excellence and in great numbers were also made in bronze and iron; bowls, knockers, inkstands, fire-dogs, candlesticks and other domestic implements either for use or ornament,

Lamp stand; Italian; sixteenth century.

of the time of the renaissance, are to be found in almost every national collection. Besides these, many small bronzes, statuettes and bas-reliefs, chiefly copied from the antique were made by the Florentine sculptors. Medallion portraits were also chased by artists of the first rank, not only in Italy but in Germany and Flanders.

Gilt metal; Italian; sixteenth century.

It would exceed our limits to attempt any enumeration of the numerous bronze works of mediæval time existing in Europe: but we must mention one or two in England; and, chief among them, the beautiful effigy in Westminster abbey of queen Eleanor, who died in 1291. This is a work of great purity and truth of conception, and of admirable execution. The head rests upon two cushions diapered in gilding with the arms of Castile and Leon, with a rich canopy of tabernacle work. The artist was Master William Torell, goldsmith and jeweller of London, who finished it in 1292. By him, also, is the effigy of Henry the third in gilded bronze, which lies next to that of queen Eleanor. At Canterbury the figure of the Black Prince, also in gilt bronze, lies upon his tomb: it is somewhat stiff but ably modelled, and the face calmly expressive. He is clothed in chain armour, and some of the details—the crown, the girdle, and the spurs—are enriched with enamel. At Warwick is the grand monument of earl Richard Beauchamp, who died in 1435.

Some of the oriental bronzes, especially the Chinese or Japanese, are admirably characteristic in design and perfect in execution. The finest Japanese are especially distinguished by extreme lightness. Some of them, being lifted, cause even a singular illusion; in first taking them into the hand one is prepared to raise a piece of metal, and it is found to be almost as light as glass. In their bronzes the Japanese have proved themselves to be, as in some other manufactures, most intelligent and expert artists. Nearly all their best works are modelled carefully first in wax, and treated in so masterly a manner, so daintily also and minutely finished with the tool, that objects comparatively common, such as baskets and small stands, are marvels of truthful reproduction.

Iron, notwithstanding its hardness, was also wrought and

chiselled, principally in Germany and especially, at Augsburg. The handles of swords and daggers, articles of furniture and still commoner utensils, were richly chased in high relief; even detached statuettes were executed in iron. One of the most celebrated examples of Augsburg work of this kind now extant is a chair made for Rodolph the second, and preserved at Longford castle near Salisbury. Many larger works were also executed in iron in the sixteenth and seventeenth centuries; such as the fine French gates of the gallery of Apollo at the Louvre and several, well known, in England.

Long before this time, however, in the middle ages artists in iron produced similar works which have never been surpassed; such, especially, as gates and hinges, knockers, and other decorations for doors. Some few examples are still to be found in this country; and we may see hinges spread out upon the panels, strengthening as well as decorating them, with a singular beauty and freedom of design.

Milanese dagger; chiselled iron.

Many of the keys also of the same period are admirably made: architectural divisions, chiselled apparently by the locksmith as easily as if the material was soft and yielding, ornament the handles or a centre boss. The mediæval fashion,

Iron bolt; French; about 1550.

Iron bolt; sixteenth century.

which lasted for several generations, of wearing "gipcieres" or pouches created a demand for decorated keys and small locks upon which no labour seems to have been spared.

A very beautiful mode of decorating iron and steel was by damascening. By this term is generally understood the art of cutting out thin plates of metal and fixing them upon another metal of different colour and usually of an inferior quality, either by pressure or by grooves previously incised upon the surface to receive them. Damascening is partly mosaic work, partly engraving, and partly carving. In the first, the pieces are inlaid; in the second, the metal is indented or cut in intaglio; in the last, gold and silver are wrought into it in relief.

Some writers have asserted that the art of true damascening was known to the ancients, and notices are to be found in the earlier classics of the ornamentation of one metal by another. The Romans under the empire undoubtedly knew the method: and some good specimens may be seen in collections; as, for example, a statuette of the time of Adrian and a pedestal (also Roman) in the British museum. Whatsoever may be the date of the invention we must refer it probably to the east, and, as the name itself would suggest, to the city or neighbourhood of Damascus.

The most famous damascened steels of Persia were those of Ispahan, Khorassan, and Shiraz. Some beautiful examples have lately been added to the Kensington museum: where a peculiar manner of damascening may be observed; produced simply by gilding the surface of the metal with gold leaf and burnishing it with an agate or other hard stone.

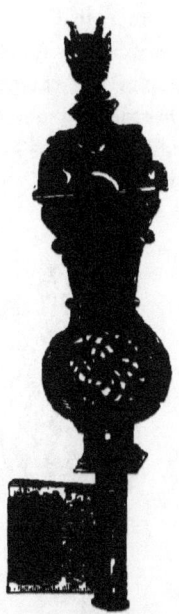

Key; 15th century.

Usually, the process of damascening differed according to the hardness of the metal. When iron was used the whole surface was covered with fine incisions, upon which the design was inlaid by means of gold or silver wires; these were fastened by strong pressure or beaten in with a hammer. The piece was then polished with a burnisher, which not only fixed the gold or silver more firmly but obliterated the incisions and restored the original polish. When finished, the damascening resembled a flat embroidery. The other varieties, spoken of above, were worked in a somewhat similar manner.

This art of damascening attained its highest perfection in

Europe in the sixteenth century: Venice and especially Milan were famous for it. Not only armour and weapons, but caskets, tables, and cabinets were damascened with ornaments and arabesques of the most exquisite devices. One of the most admirable specimens known to us of this period is the shield, attributed to Benvenuto Cellini, in the royal collection at Windsor.

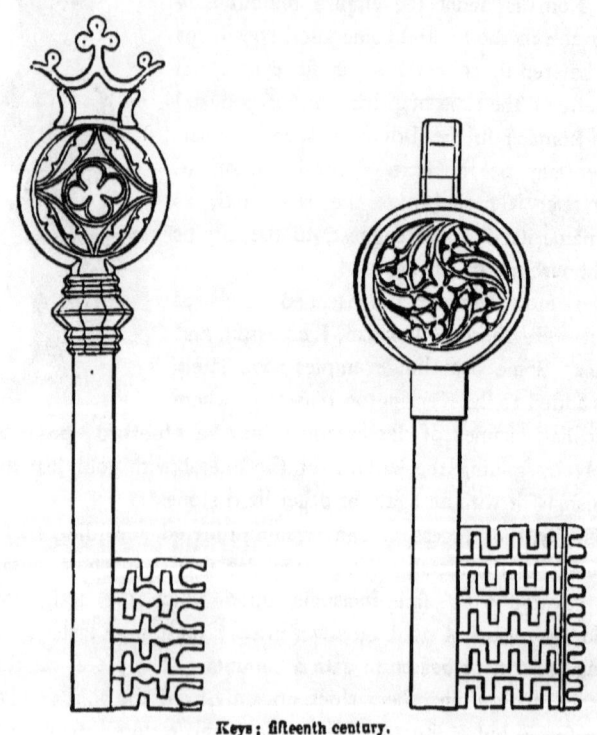

Keys; fifteenth century.

ENAMELS.

Base of a salt-cellar; Limoges; 16th century.

ENAMELS.

NAMEL is a mixed material fused and vitrified by the action of fire, and applied to the decoration of any substance; metal, stone, earthenware, or even glass. Usually, the term "an enamel" is restricted to metal work so ornamented, the one requisite being that the vitreous decoration shall have been fixed in its place by fusion. Enamel is in fact glass composed of metallic oxides to which certain fixed fusible salts have been added under heat sufficient to affect the surface to which the paste is to be permanently united. The metallic oxides give the required colours, and as these colours are liable to change under various degrees of temperature, great skill and patience are necessary to determine the exact degree, and the time also of exposure which will ensure the hue, and no other, intended by the artist. Enamels are either opaque or transparent; opacity is obtained by adding a certain quantity of oxide of tin. Opaque enamels are commonly rubbed down and polished after the process of firing is complete.

The art of enamelling is of very early date; and a rather similar mode of decoration, although it cannot be called an imitation, was employed by the old Egyptians, who greatly loved brilliant colouring. They cemented into gold cells small pieces of glass or precious stones carefully shaped; but they do not seem to have been acquainted with the art of fusing the several parts. It is true that Dr. Birch, a great authority, speaks (in his book upon ancient pottery) of "enamelled objects" as early as the fourth Egyptian dynasty, 2000 years before Christ: but in another work, describing the famous jewels of a later Egyptian queen, he accurately says that "the pastes which decorate them are not enamel, but cut into the required shapes and inlaid. The principal substances thus used were lapis lazuli, jasper, etc., or opaque glass to imitate them and the delicate blue of the turquoise. Their real enamelling does not appear to be older than the time of the Ptolemaic and Roman dominion in Egypt."

We cannot possibly say from what distant time enamelling was practised by the Chinese, but undoubtedly very long ago. The Greeks and Etruscans used enamel to enrich their jewellery, and very beautiful specimens have been found in tombs, particularly a gold necklace now in the British museum. In the Campana collection at the Louvre are some funereal crowns ornamented with small enamelled flowers; also some birds, peacocks and doves, executed with such neatness of hand as to indicate that the art was then in current practice. The process was probably the same as that of the renaissance jewels.

The first distinct mention of enamelling in any classic author is a passage in Philostratus, about A.D. 240, who speaks of a maritime people who ornamented horse-trappings by means of vitrified colours. Such horse-trappings together with various ornaments, such as brooches, bracelets, rings, etc., have been found in Britain : and we may say that the art was practised in this country, perhaps before and certainly during the Roman occupation, and in Ireland.

A remarkable altar-tray and chalice were found near Chalon-sur-Saone, in France, about thirty years ago, and are now in the public library at Paris. (See next woodcut.) These are of gold enamelled, and supposed to be of the fifth or sixth century.

The western nations of Europe carried the art of enamelling to very high perfection from the eighth or ninth century up to the sixteenth : and examples of certain kinds of work exist, about which we know neither the composition nor the method of application. It was natural then, as now, that an artist should keep secret the mystery of his success, and various curious processes died out with their inventors.

ENAMELS.

Altar tray and chalice, sixth century?

There are three distinct classes of enamels: 1, embedded or (as some say) encrusted; 2, translucent upon relief; and 3, painted.

Embedded enamels are of two kinds and we describe them by their French names, *cloisonné* and *champlevé*. Cloisonné enamels are generally small, extremely rare and valuable, and very seldom to be found in any collection. A very curious early example is preserved in Russia, of which we give a woodcut. (See next page.) The mode of making them is well given by M. Labarte. "The plate of metal intended as a foundation was first provided with a little rim to retain the enamel. Slender strips of gold of the same depth as the rim were then bent in short lengths and fashioned to form the outline of the pattern. These short bits were then fixed, upright, upon the plate.

The metal outline being thus arranged, the intervening spaces were filled with the different enamels, reduced to fine powder and moistened into a paste. The piece was then placed in the furnace, and when the fusion was complete was withdrawn with certain precautions that the cooling might be effected gradually.

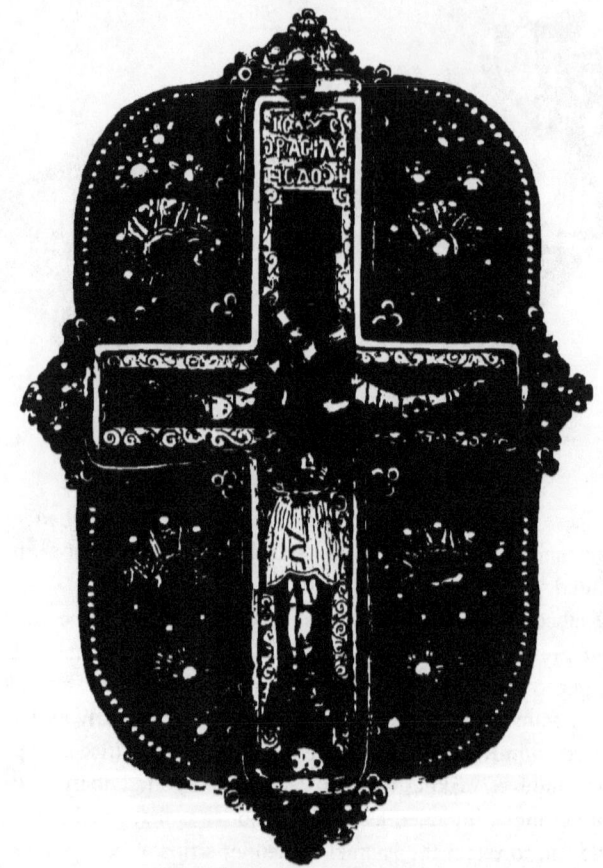

Byzantine reliquary, tenth century.

The enamel when thoroughly cold was ground and polished. It is easy to comprehend that the old artists must have used very pure gold and extremely fusible enamels, in order that the plate might not be injured from the action of the fire, or the thin strips of metal be melted by the heat which fused the paste."

Theophilus, who wrote a most valuable treatise in the tenth

century, called "Schedula diversarum artium," gives a minute description of the mode in which cloisonné enamels were made. Having spoken of the arrangement of the pattern by means of the delicate strips, he tells us in a passage worth quoting how the enamels were to be introduced. "Take," he says, "the kinds of glass which you have prepared, and breaking a particle from each piece, place the fragments upon a piece of copper, arrange the coals round and above it, and blowing carefully you will see whether they melt equally; if so, use them all; if any particle is harder than the rest, place it by itself. Taking separate pieces of the proved glass, place them in the fire, and when each glows, throw it into water and it instantly flies into small bits, which you break until made quite fine; which, having washed, you put into a clean vessel and cover with a linen cloth. The separate colours being so prepared, take a piece of the soldered gold and fasten it with wax upon a smooth table: then with a goosequill cut to a point, but not split, fill a compartment with one of the colours: and so on, until the whole piece is filled with the different coloured pastes. Taking away the wax, place the piece upon a thin iron, and cover it with another iron, hollow like a cup, and perforated finely all over, in order to stop the cinders, if by chance any should fall into it. Then arrange the coals round and above it very carefully, and blow with the bellows on every side until the coals glow equally. Waiting about half an hour, you uncover by degrees, and again wait until the holes of the iron grow black inside; then place it, covered as it is, in the furnace behind, till it has become quite cold. You will then take it out and wash it." Further directions follow as to the polishing; which is to be done by rubbing for a long time upon a hard and smooth hone, and with ingredients which he specifies.

It has been already said that cloisonné enamels are extremely rare; not only the smallness of their size but the value of the gold groundwork on which they were laid led to their destruction.

Very probably, also, there were but few artists at any time who had the skill to make them. At Paris, in the public library, are portions of the dress and arms of Childeric, who was buried late in the fifth century. These relics were found in his tomb, when opened in 1653; and are ornamented with a kind of coarse setting forming a honeycomb work, the interstices of which are filled with (some say) translucent coloured enamels. In the same collection is the cover of a manuscript probably of the seventh century, with four little cloisonné enamels of flowers, one at each corner; the colours are opaque, white, light blue, and semi-transparent green. Barbaric as some of the uses of many of the relics of remote antiquity may appear, we find that no object is too mean to be made agreeable to the eye. The same impulse which induced the old Celt or Frank to adorn himself with torques and brooches led him to decorate those objects with such fanciful ornaments as he could conceive, or his rude tools permit him to execute. An absolute freedom of individual design unquestionably prevailed. Hence out of the numberless examples of enamelled jewellery which have been found in the graves of buried chiefs, though all have a certain similarity in form, scarcely any two are identical in ornamentation. However complicated may be the system of knotwork which is the ordinary feature of the enriched compartments, each artist seems to have orginated something expressly for himself. It is this fertility of fancy, coupled often with rare dexterity in workmanship, which gives their principal charm to these old jewels, uninfluenced as they were by any directing guide of traditional style or scientific training.

Mr. Beresford Hope possesses a small pectoral cross of about the year 950, enamelled on both sides by the cloisonné process, which for some time past has been liberally lent for exhibition at South Kensington; and at Vienna are the famous crown and sword of Charlemagne. The more ancient portions of this crown and sword are of the date assigned to them, and are ornamented with figures in cloisonné enamel. The flesh tints are in rose colour;

the draperies and accessories in blue, red, and white. Our space prevents the description of a few more celebrated examples: merely mentioning the Pala d'Oro or altar front at Venice, the shrine of the three kings at Cologne, and the well-known jewel at Oxford, made (as some read the inscription) for king Alfred.

There is a kind of cloisonné enamel even more rare than the class in which we put the examples just spoken of: this is the enamel "de plique à jour," and was made without a background, imitating transparent stones or the glass panes in window tracery, set clear and melted in the framework or compartments of a net-

Cup, with translucent enamels, set transparently: Kensington museum.

work of gold, A most beautiful specimen of this admirable work is at South Kensington, a small cup.

In the champlevé enamels a slender line of metal shows on the surface the principal outlines of the design: but the outline instead of being arranged in detached pieces is formed out of a portion of the plate itself. The artist in this work having polished a piece of metal about a quarter of an inch thick, generally copper, traced upon it the outlines of his subject; then with proper tools he hollowed out all the spaces to be filled with the different enamels, leaving slender lines level with the original surface to keep them distinct. The vitreous matter, either dry or reduced to a paste was then introduced into the cavities, and fusion was effected by the same process as in the cloisonné enamels. After the piece had become cold it was polished, and the exposed lines of copper having been gilded it was returned to the fire. The gilding required only a moderate temperature, not high enough to injure the incrustations of enamel.

Champlevé enamels of almost every age for nearly the last thou-

Champlevé enamel: French: fourteenth century.

sand years are not uncommon.; unlike the gold used for the cloisonné, the cheapness of copper admitted the employment of large plates, and offered much less temptation to the melter. Nor were they easily destroyed; the material is durable, and the enamel is thickly laid upon it. Certain periods are distinguished by peculiarities: for example, flesh tints represented by enamel and colours in the draperies may be attributed to the eleventh and twelfth centuries; and to the two succeeding that manner of disposing the enamels which employed them only for giving

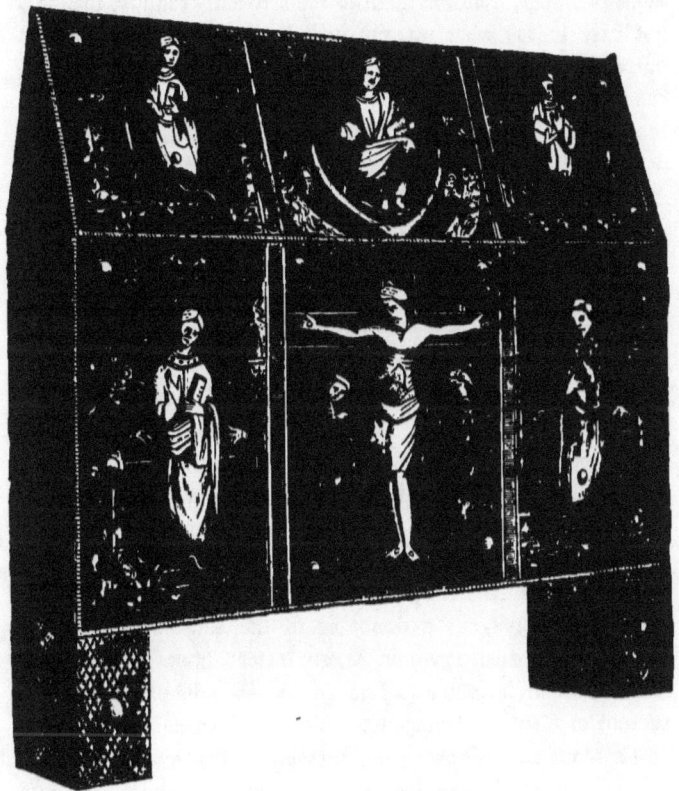

Enamelled shrine: thirteenth century.

colour to the ground, leaving the subject or figures to be expressed by fine engraving on the gilded metal, or by reliefs. Some authorities also say that there was a succession of favourite colours: in the eleventh century, blue, red of two tints, and green; in the twelfth, violet and iron-grey are added; and the use of light tones or half tints: in the next the enamel serves merely to cover the background, and blue is the prevailing colour.

So general was the decoration with this kind of enamel of all kinds of things, from the tenth to the sixteenth century, that it is not easy to say what was not included. Articles for household purposes, for ceremonial use, armour, swords, and belts; caskets, candlesticks, cups and basins; smaller objects, rings, buttons and brooches; all were commonly so ornamented. But chiefly ecclesiastical utensils and church furniture. Many rich examples of shrines, crosiers, portable altars, censers, diptychs and the like are to be seen in most of the great national collections both at home and abroad; and the references made to them in mediæval inventories and other documents are innumerable.

Portable altar: German: thirteenth century. Kensington museum.

The chief centre from whence the largest number of these enamelled pieces came, and undeniably the most important and the most sought after, was Limoges. Even now, we speak (as it were generally) of such enamels as "Limoges." The date of the first beginnings there is not known; but probably before the year 1050. There may be a doubt as to the effigy of William de Valence (who died 1129) in Westminster abbey, but we may almost certainly attribute to Limoges the splendid plaque with the portrait of Geoffry Plantagenet, which once ornamented his tomb at Le Mans and is now in the museum of that town. He died in 1151, at which time the enamel was made. About fifty years later (not to mention foreign records) we find plenty of evidence proving the established renown of Limoges work. Among the gifts of a bishop of Rochester, in 1200, are enumerated " cofres de Limoges : " pyxes of Limoges work are particularly ordered to be provided for churches in 1240, by a bishop of Worcester: and the tomb of a bishop of Rochester, about the same time, was decorated with the same quality of enamel; the accounts are still extant with the items of expenses incurred by sending a messenger to Limoges, for the price of the monument, and for the bringing it to England.

Translucent enamels upon relief were made by Italian artists about the year 1300 and grew more perfect as time went on ; reaching the highest excellence in the sixteenth century. Benvenuto Cellini gives a detailed description of the mode of preparing and applying the enamels. He says that the colours were first to be pulverised and carefully washed ; then to be dried, by pressure, as dry as possible. The enamel was then to be laid very thinly upon the surface of the relief, in order that the colours should not run one into another. In placing the piece in the furnace much caution is to be used so that the enamel might approach it gradually and be heated slowly : and afterwards as cautiously watched that it might not run. It was then to be withdrawn, and having gradually become cold another layer of enamel was applied and the same process of fusion was repeated. When the piece had again cooled the enamel was reduced in thickness until sufficiently transparent, and lastly polished.

A very beautiful example of admirable work (Italian, about the year 1580) in translucent enamel upon gold is in the South Kensington museum; a small book cover, no. 736.

The origin of painted enamels must be referred to Limoges, as well as the production of the best examples. Works of this kind accompanied the taste for translucent enamels upon the precious metals which grew rapidly after the year 1400. The earliest specimens have thick paste, sometimes partially translucent and in slight relief, with pearls and jewels on the ornamental details of the subject. The process employed differed essentially from those before described. The workman no longer required a graver; the metal was entirely concealed under the enamel, which, spread upon the surface by a pencil, expressed at the same time both the outline and the colouring.

During the fifteenth and sixteenth centuries continued improvement and some modifications of the process of painting in enamel are to be traced. Touches of gold for light parts of the hair of figures or upon the draperies and imitations of jewels became common; and enamels of this date are generally painted upon rather thick plates of copper, slightly convex to prevent warping in the fire, and coated with a thick enamel at the back. The tints in these earlier enamels are varied and exceedingly vivid, producing the effect of an illumination. At last, the Limousin enamellers were able to produce the long series of splendid works, cups, vases, ewers, and basins, salt-cellars and other table furniture, caskets and hunting-horns, large portraits and medallions, which are to be seen in every national collection and have spread their renown throughout the whole of Europe.

The great influence of Italian artists was felt in France, during the reign of Francis the first, in every branch of art-workmanship. Enamel painters were not behind the rest; and adopted with improved designs a more sober and harmonious system of colouring. Many of the best specimens of this time are merely painted in chiaroscuro, with light flesh tints. The use of *paillettes* (small raised discs of foil to imitate gems, just above referred to) was abandoned, and the plates made thinner and less convex. The designs of Raphael were frequently copied from the engravings of Marc Antonio and his followers.

This excellence of manufacture was reached not only by workman succeeding workman but by the traditions handed down in more than one family, the father followed by the son, for two and perhaps for three generations. Among these, especially,

ENAMELS.

are the famous names of Pénicaud and Courtois. One of the best pieces of Pénicaud the elder is in the museum of Cluny, in Paris, signed and dated, 1503. He was, probably, the inventor of a new variety of process: and the taste for refined and external luxury received great impulse from the desire to possess the beautiful works produced in the new school of Limoges. Enamelled dishes, ewers, coffers and caskets, soon supplanted the massive plate of gold and silver of the preceding ages: and the painter's enamel caused a great revolution in the conventional character of goldsmiths' work, garnishing the sideboards of wealthy people with furniture brilliantly decorated and enriched with colours of delicate and liquid tints.

Vase, Limoges; 16th century.

A greater artist than Pénicaud was Léonard, surnamed Limousin, whose first works are dated 1532, the last in 1574. His portraits are admirable; and the finest existing examples are in the Louvre. The general effect of his work is light and harmonious; it is relieved by bright blue tints, or turquoise blue upon a shining ground. He is specially to be distinguished by a tint of bright yellow which he puts into the hair, and by pink and limpid flesh tints. No one, also, knew better than Léonard how to make use of golden touches wherewith to ornament his medallions or his designs upon a dark ground. His contemporary, Pierre Raymond, is scarcely inferior to Léonard.

A coarse kind of champlevé enamel on brass seems to have been made in England in Elizabeth's reign; light and dark blue and white inlaid in the interstices of a pattern in relief. Fire-dogs have been preserved of this work; and there are two candlesticks at South Kensington.

Portions of a salt-cellar; by Pierre Raymond.

The names of many enamellers of the Limousin are known; but their art began to decline about 1650; and after the reign of Louis the fourteenth fell into complete decay. A coarse colouring and an uncertain outline characterize the last period of Limoges enamels.

A new method of applying enamel, however, rose with the decline of the old: and a discovery attributed to Jean Toutin, a French goldsmith, was the beginning of a process which was soon carried by his pupils, and especially by Petitot, to most wonderful perfection. By this method opaque vitrifiable colours were laid (the plate being gold) upon a thin ground of enamel, and passed through the fire with scarcely any change in their tints. These opaque colours were applied upon the enamel ground, in the same way as water colours are laid upon ivory. Many of the miniature portraits executed in this manner for about a hundred years after 1620 by a number of known artists, both French and German, are extremely good; but the name of Petitot stands above them all. No one has ever equalled the delicacy of his drawing or the spirit and the skill of his colouring. Some of the portraits which he painted are scarcely larger than a sixpence; yet the merit of the design and the precision with which it is traced, the clearness with which the features are defined, and the perfection of execution, leave scarcely an opening for criticism. Petitot almost always enamelled upon gold; a metal which suffers least in the often repeated exposure to the heat of the furnace.

The mode of enamelling adopted by Petitot was applied by other artists to many small objects of personal luxury and ornament. Snuff-boxes, watch-cases, rings and little work-cases were beautifully decorated with scenes of battles, or rural dances and the like; or with flowers and fruit and animals; all designed and finished in a manner so charming that, unfortunately, modern artists fall far short of reaching it; though we trust that the future may some day once more give us both the genius to design and the hand to execute.

The working palette of an enamel painter is extremely rich in colours. Metallic oxides readily lend themselves to an infinite number of combinations with glass. The green, blue, red, turquoise, greys, orange, and yellow, are to be obtained either pure or compound, so as to form shades as gradual as a chromatic scale. The light red colour is called in old books upon the subject "the chief and paragon of all." It is said to have been discovered by a goldsmith who studied alchemy and found it one day at the bottom of his crucible, in trying to make gold.

Unfortunately all these kinds are not equally fusible. It is therefore necessary that the workman should be thoroughly acquainted with the precise degree of temperature that each will stand without melting too much and running one into another. When this knowledge is acquired, he places the very hardest first, then the hard, and so on. The same plate may be subjected to the furnace as often as twenty times; and we can imagine therefore the risk and the difficulty of a successful result.

About the middle of the last century a small factory was set up at Battersea, and many painters in enamel were employed; it lasted perhaps for thirty years. Some good examples of the work produced there are in the South Kensington collection; and also of some made at Bilston, in Staffordshire.

Candlestick; Battersea enamel; Kensington museum.

FURNITURE.

A royal dinner table, from a manuscript of the fourteenth century.

FURNITURE.

AS mere objects for private collections it is not usual to gather together pieces of furniture. Very beautiful and important examples are to be found in royal palaces both in England and abroad, and in private houses: but these have either descended from father to son, or have been purchased as required, either as splendid decorations for rooms or for common use. Such a collection as that at South Kensington has been made in order to direct attention to the best specimens which can be obtained of various periods, especially of the last three centuries; and so in this branch of the fine arts also, to improve modern taste by giving opportunities of examining the carving and ornaments, or the skill and ingenuity of the workmanship.

In the museum may be seen chests, cabinets, caskets, chairs, bedsteads, and tables of various kinds which have been used in England, France, Germany, and Italy since the beginning of the fifteenth century and, in a few cases, of even earlier date. There are reproductions also of the furniture of more remote times, such as the chair of Dagobert, illustrating old manners through many generations of the "dark ages," up to the luxurious civilization of the Greeks and Romans, as revealed to us in the discoveries at Pompeii and Herculaneum.

There is much evidence still existing of the kind and style of furniture which was used among the earliest nations of the world which are known in history. The painted tombs and sculptured monuments of Egypt and Nineveh show us the forms of their chairs, their tables, and their couches. In the British museum are preserved some still existing examples of chairs and footstools. The ornaments employed in both those ancient countries seem to

FURNITURE.

Stool; in sculpture, from Nineveh.

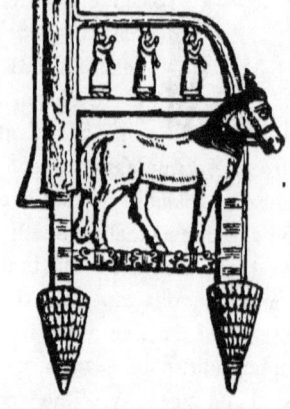
Chair; in bas-relief, from Nineveh.

have been chiefly inlaying of other woods, or metal, or ivory, and ebony. At Nineveh the legs ended commonly with the feet of some animal, probably in bronze.

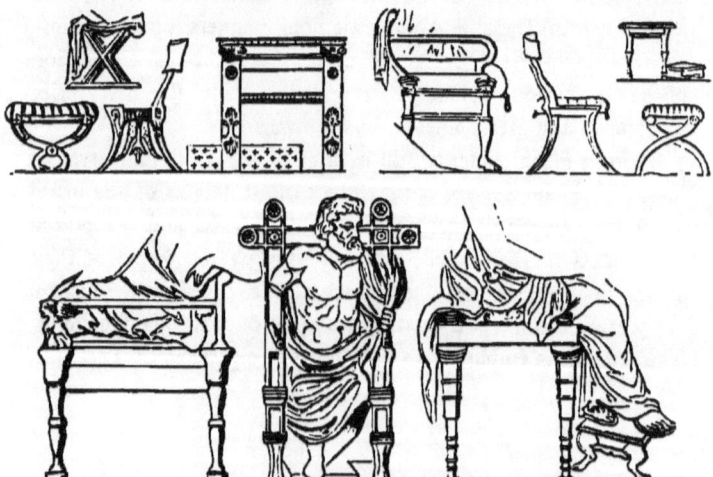
Greek chairs from bas-reliefs.

FURNITURE.

The oldest remaining models of Greek furniture to which we can refer are in the British museum; the chairs on which the figures in the Syrian room are seated. These are of the date of nearly six centuries before Christ. They represent chairs of wood with backs, perpendicular before and behind. The frame pieces of the seats are morticed into the legs, and the mortices and tenons are clearly marked in the marble, the horizontal passing through the upright bars. The Greeks also had arm-chairs and folding chairs of metal: they used couches for sleeping on, but

Greek couches.

not (as the Romans) for reclining on at meals. Their tables were of wood, marble, and metal; and the supports either lion or leopard legs and heads, or sphinxes with lifted wings.

The Romans, in imperial times, were luxurious in the furniture and fittings of their houses, as in their other habits and manners. The ornamental woodwork in their rooms was often extremely rich, and paintings, mosaics, and statues were hung upon the walls or filled the principal apartments. The doors and ceilings were gilded, or inlaid with ivory and coloured woods. Among their ornamental furniture especially were candelabra, and very elegant tripods, three-legged frames supporting tables or braziers. Original examples of these may be seen in the British museum. Their tables must have been very beautiful, and were made of marble, silver, or bronze; of ivory or of wood inlaid with ivory; damascened or otherwise enriched with the precious

Roman tripod.   Roman candelabrum.

metals. They had an infinite variety of benches, chairs, stools and couches. It may give some notion of the expense incurred

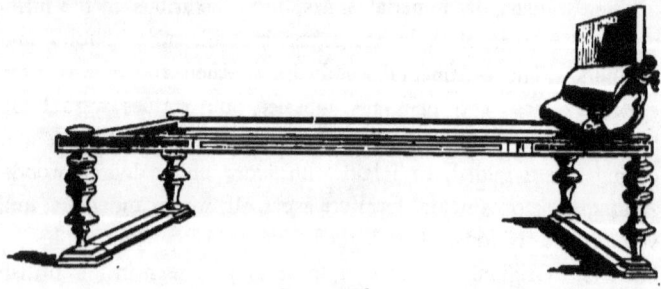

Roman couch.

in making some of their finest furniture, when we remember that tables are recorded by historians which cost £9000.

FURNITURE.

We have but few memorials and still fewer examples existing of the furniture used in Europe after the break up of the Roman empire. During the succeeding eight or ten centuries the incessant state of war and struggle which prevailed, not only in Italy but in the west, was naturally destructive of all personal wealth, and of the means even of obtaining or preserving costly furniture. The fashion of the few pieces of any kind which are still extant took their origin and followed the forms in use at Constantinople; and, in a general way, are in style Byzantine.

The chair (so called) of St. Peter, kept in the church of St. Peter at Rome, is probably the most ancient and interesting relic of furniture in existence. It is made of wood, overlaid with carved ivory and gold. The back is composed of little columns and arches, with a pedimental top. The tradition is that it was part of the furniture of the house of the senator Pudens, who is mentioned in St. Paul's epistles. Another celebrated chair, brought in 1204 from Constantinople where it had been kept for ages, is preserved at Venice in the treasury of St. Mark's. The chair of St.

Chair of St. Peter.

Maximian at Ravenna dates from the sixth century. In the collection of the Louvre, at Paris, is a famous chair, traditionally said to have been made for king Dagobert, about the year 630. This is of bronze and has been gilt: it is of two dates, the upper portion of the arms having been added in the beginning of the twelfth century. A copy of the chair is in the South Kensington museum.

Soon after the year 1000 we can perceive an improvement in

Chair of Dagobert.

almost every art; but England down to the time of the Norman conquest scarcely kept pace with other countries. The furniture of Anglo-saxon houses (which usually consisted of only one story) was rude and simple: and, judging from illuminations in contemporary manuscripts, it often took the form of animals. Generally, a heavy table and benches seem to have comprised all the requirements of the living-rooms, and even bedsteads were not used except by the ladies or

Bedstead; eleventh century.

chief people of the family. Curtains, however, and wall hangings were not uncommon decorations.

A great advance, however, was made in all articles of domestic use and for comfort or luxury before the end of the thirteenth century when, both in England and on the continent, what we call mediæval art reached its highest perfection. Panelled framework came into use, especially for cabinets and chests: and these were decorated with all sorts of enrichments. A chest of the time of king John, ornamented with hammered iron plates and hinges, is preserved at Rockingham. The halls and large rooms of castles and great houses were lighted with chandeliers of iron, and furnished with chairs, settles and benches. Bedrooms were wainscoted and hung with painted cloths or tapestry, and provided with seats

Seats, fourteenth century.

and closets for hanging linen and for keeping stores.

Bedroom, fourteenth century.

We often see in the illuminations of manuscripts of this period chests used as tables, especially for games, such as chess. The long seats in the principal room are shown with high raised backs as a protection from the wind, and in the form of the settle so long and still in use in country inns and farm houses. The better class of such settles was fitted with a rich canopy over the heads of the people sitting, carved and panelled. Tables were made in a fashion more according to our own time, and were no longer mere boards laid upon trestles and easily removable. A very fine octagonal table of this date is preserved in the chapter-house of Salisbury cathedral. We engrave also a round table, from a manuscript of the fourteenth century.

Round table of the fourteenth century.

FURNITURE.

The quantity of hangings and tapestry of various kinds used from the 14th to the 16th century in fitting up houses was prodigious: and no surer proof can be given than the abundance which was always forthcoming to decorate the streets of a town when a procession was to pass. The contemporary chronicles are full of records of such modes of showing reverence and welcome.

Among the pieces of mediæval furniture which still remain the coronation chair in Westminster abbey, made in the reign of Edward the first, is the most important and of especial interest. This is of oak, with straight supports and sides, flat seat, and gable back. The sides and back are decorated with carved panels: and the gable is crocketed, with pinnacles. The wood has been fastened together with pins and was originally covered with a coat of plaster which was afterwards gilded. Indistinct traces may still be seen of a sort of diaper of quatrefoils filled with figures, grotesques, etc., with which the back was once ornamented.

The coronation chair.

There are several very fine mediæval chests in the South Kensington collection: especially some examples of Italian furniture

English folding stool; fifteenth century.

of that kind. These were generally gilt and painted; and the richness of the work, which is often remarkable, is owing to the careful preparation of the ground on which the gold is laid, and the way in which it was modelled with the tool. The old gold was thickly laid on, very pure, and malleable; less liable therefore to suffer from the action of the atmosphere than the gold which we now use. The paintings executed on such chests, so prepared, were by the hand of some of the best artists of the time.

Reading desk; Italian, fifteenth century.

Another mode of ornamentation was introduced by the Venetians from India and Persia about the end of the fourteenth century, and specimens, particularly in the shape of small caskets and moderate-sized chests, not unfrequently occur. This decoration is a kind of marquetry, an inlay of ivory, metal, and woods, stained to vary the colour, and always in geometric patterns. Some handsome chairs are at South Kensington, made about the year 1500, inlaid in this manner.

In the west of Europe the introduction and adoption of decorated furniture became rapidly more and more widely spread during the fifteenth century: and the splendour which had hitherto been chiefly limited to ecclesiastical purposes and church utensils was to be seen also in domestic life. When the wars of the Roses ceased in England, a great increase of trade and riches succeeded, and with it a corresponding

FURNITURE.

growth in luxury. With the beginning of the reign of Henry the seventh we may connect the formation of new tastes and new requirements in English society; and, keeping pace with other signs of wealth and prosperity, the royal palaces and the great houses in cities and in the country became filled with magnificent furniture. Foreign artists were sent for and employed to make designs or to execute the work.

In whatever year we might be inclined to place the beginning of the renaissance period we may very properly include within it the whole of the sixteenth century. The best examples of renaissance furniture are undoubtedly Italian, and the influence of that style is to be seen in the contemporary furniture of England, France, and Germany. The Italian artists used wood chiefly in their tables, cabinets, chairs, etc : and decorated it with gilding, painting and sculpture; or with inlays of agate, lapis lazuli, ivory, tortoiseshell, and mother-of-pearl. Smaller objects, such as mirrors, were made of iron or other metal and richly damascened.

Italian chair; sixteenth century.

The earlier Italian inlaid work was, as already said, in geometric patterns : but about the year 1500 we find figure designs introduced. This was done at first in two or three woods only, usually in pine and cypress. The large grain was employed to express lines of drapery and other movements by putting whole portions of a dress or figure with the grain in one direction or another, as required. This sort of work is called "tarsia" or

Sculpture, ou Italian chest.

"intarsiatura"; and is, in fact, a kind of mosaic in woods. The subjects most proper for tarsia work are perspective representations of buildings full of windows and angular lines, to which force and relief are given by means of lights and shades. Very fine examples may be seen in the interior fittings of the sacristies and choirs of many Italian churches.

Another, and very beautiful method of ornamentation was the "pietra dura" or mosaic panelling of hard stones: an exceedingly laborious and costly work. The materials are the precious marbles, such as agate, carnelian, lapis lazuli, or amethyst; and each part must be ground to an exact shape and the whole fitted accurately together. Besides being formed into panels for table tops and cabinet fronts "pietra dura" was let into wood, and with its bright colours helped the sombre tone of the walnut or ebony base.

A feature strongly developed in sixteenth century furniture is the architectural character of its outlines. In the fifteenth century chests, screens, stall fronts, doors and panelling followed the prevailing arrangements of design in the stone work, such as window tracery and the like. But in the furniture of the reigns of Henry the seventh and eighth and queen Mary an architectural character, not proper to woodwork for any constructive reasons, was given to cabinets, chests, etc. They were artificially provided with parts that imitated the lines, the brackets, and other details of classic entablatures, which have not the same propriety when reduced to the dimensions of furniture. These subdivisions

FURNITURE.

brought into use the art of "Joinery." The parts necessary for the purpose of framing up wood, whether a table or a couch, a piece of panelling or a chair, offer opportunities for mouldings

English, fifteenth century.

Flemish, sixteenth century.

Panels.

French, sixteenth century.

German, fifteenth century.

and carvings. Some of these are proper to the thicker portions forming the frames, some to the thin flat boards that fill up the spaces. To add a variety of mouldings in making cabinets or coffers, such as subdivide the roofs or peristyles of temples, is a departure from the carpenter's province and work, and impresses upon furniture another character by taking it out of its natural and obvious shape.

The fine Italian style of the renaissance was widely imitated in England, as in France, during the first half of the sixteenth century; mixed, however, not seldom with a Holbeinesque character. The beautiful "Tudor cabinet" at South Kensington is a good example of this. The panelling of halls and chambers, as of cabinets and other furniture, still retained very commonly the upright lines and mouldings of the earlier (so called) "linen" pattern. Leafwork and heads, or busts of reigning sovereigns or ancient heroes, filled the more ornamental sections of the woodwork, giving a certain classical element which was soon further developed. Much of the decorations of English furniture up to 1550 has a Flemish rather than an Italian character. This expanded into a

Small cabinet for jewels: French, in the style of Jean Goujon.

distinct English style during Elizabeth's reign, and fell back into the older fashion under Charles the first.

In France the renaissance art advanced far beyond that of England. Francis the first invited famous artists from Florence, and aimed at rivalling Florentine luxuries and refinements in the furniture and decorations of rooms no less than in other things. Jean Goujon stands at the head of the French masters, pupils of the Italian teachers. A very beautiful French table of this date is in the South Kensington museum, No. 7216'60.

French table; sixteenth century.

The furniture of the latter half of the sixteenth and beginning of the seventeenth century still kept up much of its architectural character. Cabinets, for instance, were heavy in design; and in the mouldings, instead of simple running lines worked with the plane as in mediæval woodwork, we see the egg and tongue, dentils, acanthus leaves, and other members of classical architecture, constantly repeated. The ornaments at this period show also a fondness for conventional bands interspersed with figures and other decorations.

Elizabethan is the name commonly given to a style well known, not only in architecture but in all kinds of works of art which

French cabinet; sixteenth century.

developed during her reign. Large pieces of furniture were ornamented with arabesques, or with panels and flat mouldings carved with "strapwork," a combination of ribands or straps in various folds and contortions. These were often intermixed with flowers, fruits, and tendrils. Heraldry, also, with its rich mant-

Panel from a room; about 1590; English.

lings and quaint escutcheons (the edges notched and rolled about as if made of the notched edges of a scroll of parchment) supplied frequent ornaments. Grotesque terminal figures, human headed, supported the front of the dresser in the dining-room, or of the cabinet. Table supports grew into heavy acorn-shaped pedestals. Inlaid work began to be used, and woods of various colour were inlaid in oak. The heads and testers of bedsteads, chests fronts and cabinets, were thus ornamented. The style is usually somewhat coarse, and fine examples are extremely rare. There is a piece at South Kensington; and one of the best is preserved in a house in Cornwall, dated 1592; a chest with a rich marquetry front and sides in coloured inlaid wood.

From about 1550 to 1700 the Italians carved soft woods with extraordinary grace and vigour. The frames of pictures and mirrors, as well as some of the details of cabinets, were cut out in great sweeping acanthus leaves, showing wonderful ease and certainty of execution. Chairs were made in the same style. Venice maintained for a long time a pre-eminence in this kind of carved and gilded furniture, in a greater degree even than Florence: and especially for their famous looking-glasses which found their way all over Europe.

Venetian mirror frame.

About this period marquetry began to be extensively used: and became a leading feature of furniture decoration. Mere inlaying had long been practised, but the new marquetry was a

FURNITURE.

much more artistic and picturesque composition. In England, in the reign of William and Mary, a large quantity of furniture was imported from Holland with Dutch marquetry; and houses were filled with bandy legged chairs, upright clock fronts, secretaires or bureaux, and heavy cabinets. The older designs on work of this kind represent tulips and other flowers, foliage, or birds, all

Chair; about 1690.

in gay colours, with sometimes salient points in ivory or mother-of-pearl.

With the introduction of marquetry into such general use we recognise not only an improved method of decoration but a changed ideal of construction. Chairs, tables, chests, and cabinets were conceived as such. They were no longer subdivided by architectural mouldings and other useless work added to the sides and fronts. The gradual decay also of good sculptors in wood, who were so essential in the earlier work of a hundred years before, helped the progress of another kind of ornamentation which required undoubtedly excellent workmanship but could be executed on plain surfaces.

The famous Boule marquetry was also introduced in France at nearly the same time, about 1680, by André Charles Boule. This peculiar kind of veneered work is composed chiefly of tortoiseshell and thin brass. At first, the inlay was made at great cost, owing to the waste of valuable material in cutting, and the shell was left of its natural colour. Afterwards, the manufacture was more economical. Two or three thicknesses of the material were glued together, and sawn through at one operation. An equal number of matrices or hollow pieces exactly corresponding were thus obtained and, by counterchanging, two or more designs were given by the same sawing. These are technically known as "boule and counter," the brass forming alternately the ground and the pattern. The brass was often elaborately chased with a graver.

A revival of wood carving took place about the year 1700 in England and was carried to the highest pitch of perfection by Grinling Gibbons. He carved birds, foliage, fruits, and figures with astonishing dexterity. Specimens may be seen over the communion table of St. James's church, Westminster, and in the choir of St. Paul's. The finest examples, probably, are at Petworth and Chatsworth. The foliage of his garlands and the flowers sweep round in bold and harmonious curves, and no work was ever more free from conventional arrangements.

From the beginning of the eighteenth century the best furniture generally followed the French taste : and boule work especially grew into larger structures as it passed into the hands of a greater number of workmen. The broken and fantastic forms of curve (emblems of the affected manners of the day) called Rococo from *rocaille coquille*, rock and shell curves, were well calculated to show off the lustre of the gilding which extensively prevailed. Much furniture of that time was bombé, or rolled about in curious undulations of the surface, partly to display the skill of the cabinet maker, partly on account of the marquetry, its only ornament.

In England about the time of George the second there was a large school of excellent carvers and makers of furniture. The most prominent name is that of Thomas Chippendale. He seems to have aimed at maintaining the then fashionable style with certain differences by which we may now recognise his work. His furniture is usually in mahogany; the tables, cabinets, dinner-trays etc., following architectural moulding lines such as are seen in the buildings of Sir William Chambers and the brothers Adam. During the same reign there was a favourite class of furniture of which the decorations consisted of panels of old Chinese and Japanese lac-work. These were fitted, like the marquetry of the day, with rich gilt metal mounts.

No furniture has ever excelled that made in France during the brilliant period of the reign of Louis the sixteenth. Two artists are especially famous; Riesener as a cabinet-maker, and Goutière as a maker of gilt metal mounts. Riesener used chiefly rosewood, tulip, maple, and laburnum. Wreaths and bundles of flowers, exquisitely finished and boldly designed, form the centres of his marquetry panels, which are often plain surfaces of one wood. On the sides, in borders and compartments, we find diaper patterns in three or four quiet colours. Gouthière worked with Riesener and his contemporary, David Roentgen: all their best pieces are finished with his mounts. The gilding on these mounts is so good and has been laid on so massively that the old metal work has in general suffered no material injury down to our own time, and needs but little to restore it to its original lustre. A magnificent cabinet is in the royal collection at Windsor. No signature has been found on this, although Riesener's name is commonly stamped upon some panel or part of the oak lining: but the admirable modelling of the flower borders and the perfection of the mounts leave no doubt that the makers were Riesener and Gouthière.

The pseudo-classical style of furniture which prevailed about seventy years ago, and the weak and miserable imitations of so-called "Gothic" which soon afterwards followed, have happily died away: and we may hope to see a revival of a better school of artists in consequence of the many collections of fine furniture—the shrines and carved work of the middle ages; the chests and caskets of the fifteenth century; the cabinets, chairs, and tables of the renaissance; the splendid marquetry and boule of the reigns of Louis the fifteenth and his successor; the exquisite carving of the days of queen Anne;—which have been exhibited from time to time during the last twenty years, or which are now gathered together at the South Kensington museum.

An English table and chairs of the year 1633, from a woodcut of that date.

Open work panel; fourteenth century.

(M. P. A.

IVORIES.

I N the strict meaning of the word no substance except the tusk of the elephant should be called ivory: for that, alone, presents the true characteristic, namely, a tooth substance which shows lines of different shades of colour proceeding in the arc of a circle, and forming minute curvilinear lozenge-shaped spaces. But other animals furnish what is commonly, and not improperly, spoken of as ivory; such as the walrus, the narwhal, and the hippopotamus. There is also the fossil ivory, not really fossil, but so named as being the tusk of an extinct elephant or mammoth which once roamed over the greater part of Europe. This fossil ivory is chiefly now found in the icy regions of Siberia.

No works known to us from the hand of man can claim so high an antiquity, and except some rude implements none more high than carvings in ivory and bone. They have been found in the cave dwellings of people who lived when the reindeer and the mammoth ranged over the plains of southern Europe. Incised sketches and carvings in low relief of various beasts prove to us

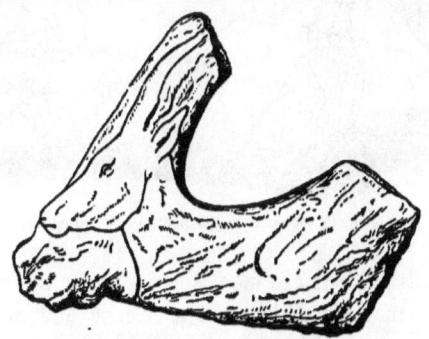
Prehistoric carving upon bone.

IVORIES.

Reindeer, drawn upon slate: prehistoric.

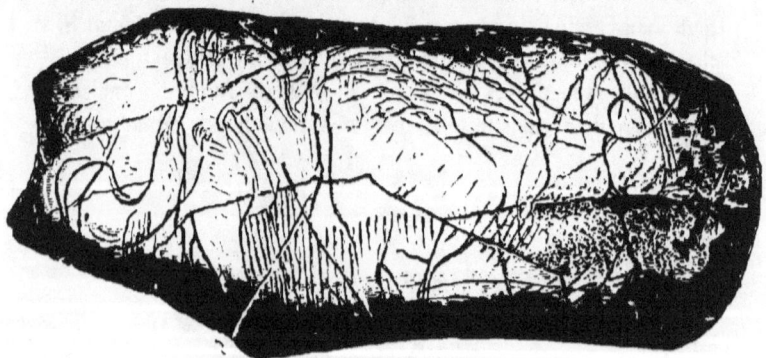

The mammoth, incised upon mammoth ivory: prehistoric.

that thousands of years ago men possessed the power of representing what they saw with the right feeling and in an artistic spirit. So important in many respects are these wonderful relics of a mysterious age that we give three woodcuts, copied from objects found at Le Moustier in the Dordogne. These show us the head and shoulder of an ibex; a group of reindeer; and outlines of the famous mammoth itself.

From these we must pass at one bound, across an interval of time the extent of which we know not how to calculate, to a period comparatively modern, although reaching back as far as the days of the Jewish monarchy and the earliest reigns of the Egyptian Pharaohs. We can point to no extant example of undoubted Jewish work; but we have sufficient evidence from the old Scriptures that ivory was largely used by that nation for purposes of decoration. Solomon (we read) "made a great throne of ivory;" and the prophets speak of "benches of ivory," of "horns of ivory," and of "beds of ivory."

Egypt, however, has left us in her tombs remains of works in ivory which date as far back as the time of Moses and Joseph. These are, of course, exceedingly rare; partly because of their fragile nature, partly because of the smallness of their size, owing to which they must have been frequently thrown aside. The British museum has a considerable collection; among them are inlaid chairs and daggers, the handle of a mirror, a painter's palette, boxes, and a statuette. At Paris, in the Louvre, is a small box with a name on it of a dynasty before the event of the Exodus.

Somewhat later than the statuette just mentioned come the famous Assyrian ivories, found at Nineveh, which are also preserved in the British museum. There are more than fifty of these; carved probably between the eleventh and the sixth century before the Christian era. Remains of gold leaf with which they were originally decorated still adhere to some of them, and Mr. Layard in his detailed account truly says that they are "elegant in design, elaborate in execution, and show an intimate knowledge of the method of working in ivory. The spirit of the design and the delicacy of the workmanship are equally to be admired."

There can be no doubt that from the year 1000 B.C., there was a constant succession of artists in ivory in the west of Asia, in Greece, and in Italy. Long before ivory was applied to the making of bas-reliefs and statues it was employed for a multitude of objects of luxury and ornament. Inferior to marble in whiteness, and as we know greatly inferior in available extent of surface, ivory exceeds marble in beauty of polish and is less fragile, being an animal substance and of true tissue and growth. From the age of Hesiod or Homer numerous allusions are to be found to various works in this material; such as the ornaments of shields, couches, and articles of domestic use. A little later, we have records of larger carvings and of statues. The most famous of these were of a mixed kind; commonly called chryselephantine, of gold or other metal and of ivory: in size so large that the figure of Minerva in the Parthenon was nearly forty feet in height, and of Jupiter at Olympia more than fifty. The faces and the uncovered parts of the bodies of these colossal statues were made of large plaques of ivory, carefully joined. Many of these splendid works existed until about the year 750; and Pausanias, who travelled through Greece in the second century, describes cabinets and chests, statues, tables and thrones made of or decorated with carvings in ivory. We must deeply regret the destruction of the statues; and the more so, as it was owing to the wilful and mad violence of Christian fanatics: the sect of the image-breakers or iconoclasts. The few remains which have come down to us from the best periods of Greek art are small, and cannot even with certainty be attributed to artists working in Greece itself. The best and the most valuable have been found in Etruscan tombs; and neither the beauty nor the wonderful spirit of the execution of them has perhaps ever been equalled in after time. The British museum may be said to be rich in the possession of some twenty or thirty examples.

Passing onwards to the Roman imperial times, we still find that ivory carvings before Constantine are almost equally scarce. Ivory and metal—the one from its nature, the other from its preciousness—have perished under conditions which have left uninjured fragile vases. Nevertheless some few remarkable pieces have been preserved. One of them, perhaps the most beautiful antique ivory in the world, is in the collection at South Kensington. It is one leaf of a diptych, nearly 12 inches long by 5 wide, upon which is carved in low relief an admirable figure of a Bacchante, with a young girl attending her: the date may be as early as the end of the second century. Another, rather later, is in the British museum; Bellerophon on horseback, executed in open work; and two more, very celebrated (also of the third century), are in the public museum at Liverpool. These last represent Æsculapius and Hygieia.

From the middle of the fourth century downwards we have an unbroken chain of examples still existing;

Leaf of Roman diptych, second century.

and we can point to carved ivories of every century, in gradually increasing numbers, which may be seen in museums in England and abroad. Their importance with reference to the history of art cannot be overrated; there is no such chain in manuscripts, or mosaics, or textiles, or gems, or enamels. The material itself or the decorations with which other works were surrounded very probably led to their destruction; and we may thank the valueless character of many a piece of carved ivory, except as a work of art, for its preservation to our own days.

The most important ivories before the seventh century are what are called "consular diptychs." Anything doubly folded is a diptych, from the old Greek word for double; and was anciently chiefly applied to tablets for writing upon. The consular diptychs were ceremonial presents, sent by the Roman consuls on their appointment to official persons or to friends. About twenty-five such diptychs, in some cases only one leaf of the pair, are known. The earliest is of the year 248, and the latest of 541; and this happens to be one of those carved for the last consul, Basilius. These diptychs being so rare are of great value, and every collection is proud if in the possession of an example. Single leaves of two are at South Kensington; a complete one in the museum at Liverpool, with a leaf also which may have been consular; and a leaf is in the British museum for which some authorities claim the same honour. The consular diptychs, having ascertained dates, are of the highest importance to the student; and we can trace the

Angel, in the British museum.

IVORIES.

rapid decline of art in the succession which spreads over more than two centuries. The earliest are the best; but even in the last we can still find a certain grandeur in the figures which shows that the better models of an older time were followed by the sculptors.

Before we pass to the large series of ivory carvings executed between the eighth and the fifteenth centuries, we must direct the reader's attention to a superb leaf in the British museum, representing an angel, in relief, of perhaps the end of the fourth century. (See p. 6.) The size of the ivory is remarkable; more than sixteen inches in length, by nearly six in width: and few antique carvings surpass this in grandeur of design, in power of expression, or in excellence of workmanship.

We must here remark that it is difficult to suggest any way in which the very large slabs, or plaques, of ivory used by the ancients were obtained. Some have thought that they knew a method, long lost, of bending, softening, and flattening solid blocks; others suppose that they were able to procure larger tusks than can be got from the degenerate animal of our day. Be this as it may, pieces of the size above mentioned (and larger specimens possibly exist)

Cup, in the British museum.

could not be cut even from the enormous pair of tusks which were exhibited in 1851, and which weighed together 325 lbs.

In the public collections both at home and abroad may be seen many examples of carved ivories from the fifth century to the time of Charlemagne, A.D. 800. The woodcut (p. 7) represents one of the most important works known of this period: a cup in the British museum. This was made not later than the year 600, and for some sacred purpose. The loose ring round the foot probably carried a thin veil to be thrown over the whole for further security and reverence.

Unlike this vase, which is good both in design and execution, the early ivories of western Europe are rude and some of them even barbarous; but early in the ninth century in consequence of the influx of Greek artists the style advanced with a very evident progression. There was a brief check about the year 1000; and then again followed a distinct improvement; impressed however with a feeling peculiar to the next hundred years. We find the figures simply designed, although in stiff and unnatural positions; the draperies close and clinging, and broken up into numerous little folds; ornamented often very largely with small jewels or beads. The school of the lower Rhine kept itself to a certain degree free from these faults; their figures preserved more movement, the modelling was better, and the draperies disposed with greater art.

As Christianity spread over western Europe ivory came to be more and more used, and especially for the decoration of ecclesiastical furniture, covers of books, and reliquaries. Diptychs were made enriched with subjects taken from the Scriptures or the lives of saints: pyxes also or boxes for consecrated wafers, retables or moveable screens to be placed on altars, holy-water buckets, handles for fans, espiscopal combs, pastoral staffs, and the like.

But the use of ivory was not confined to church and pious purposes. It was adopted for numberless things of common life among the wealthy. Caskets and coffers, hilts of weapons, mirror cases, toilet combs, writing tables, book-covers, and chessmen, were largely inlaid or made of it. Examples of each of these kinds are to be found at South Kensington. We give also woodcuts of two of the sides of a most important English casket

Two sides of casket, in the British museum.

of the eighth century in the British museum, given to the nation by Mr. Franks. The carvings are from both sacred and profane subjects, with Runic inscriptions.

About the eleventh century we find a style of carving which is apt to mislead and about which there has been much discussion. The type is classical; and some of the specimens are executed in a manner which would lead one to place them as early as the time of the Roman emperors. But there can be little doubt, if any, that they are the work of an Italian school, which lasted for a short time and copied the sculptures of the old sarcophagi and other monuments. A very fine example is "the Veroli casket" at South Kensington: and of this and similiar pieces we may say with Mr. Nesbitt that "they are characterised by peculiarities and mannerisms; among these are an exaggerated slenderness of limb, a marked prominence of the knee joints, and a way of rendering the hair by a mass of small knobs."

The ivory caskets of the middle ages were richly decorated with subjects sometimes from the Bible, more often from profane legends. The famous romances and poems supplied endless subjects: and the histories of king Arthur, or of Lancelot and Guinivere, or the adventures of Aristotle and Virgil in their character of magicians, frequently occur. The panels are sometimes decorated also with very graceful open work; as in the woodcut, two small pieces from a large series of the life of St. Agnes.

Small panels in open work.

Bone, as well as ivory, was occasionally used: especially for the marriage coffers once commonly given in Italy. As these were often of considerable size, bone was employed as being less costly: but the workmanship is not seldom that of artists of the highest eminence. The beautiful predella at South Kensington is an admirable specimen; and the woodcut represents a curious

Cover of a box.

cover of English work, with morrice dancers in the compartments.

Toilet implements, and particularly portable mirror cases and combs were plentiful. The hand mirrors of the middle ages were

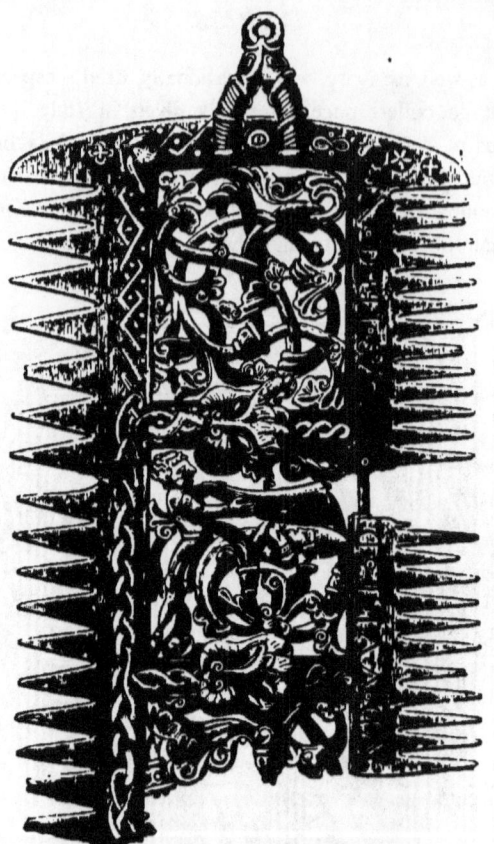

Comb, English, eleventh century, in the British museum.

Italian comb, sixteenth century.

IVORIES.

small, both of metal and of glass, and generally circular. The subject of the decoration was very often from a romance, or from the story of the castle of Love; or ladies and gentlemen riding

Mirror case.

Chessman, twelfth century. Chessman, in the British museum.

through a wood; or (almost the sole subject from Scripture) the message of David to Bathsheba. Combs were ornamented in a similar manner.

Arm of a chair, twelfth century.

English, eleventh century.

Chessmen and draughtsmen were made of ivory from very early times. A tolerably complete and most famous set is in the British museum, found in Scotland; of one like them we give a woodcut (p. 13): and of another, somewhat later in date and richly decorated with a number of figures.

The style of carving common in the eleventh and twelfth centuries is well shown in the remarkable piece, also engraved, formerly in the Meyrick collection: an arm of a chair, with interlacing scroll ornament, in which men and animals are intertwined.

IVORIES. 109

The heads of pastoral staffs and croziers of the middle ages

French, fourteenth century.

were very often made of ivory; and two examples are annexed. One, probably English; and the other French. We see in the volute of the last how cleverly the mediæval artist managed to arrange different subjects on the opposite sides: on one is the Crucifixion, on the other the Virgin and Child. A most admirable piece is in the British museum, which probably once formed the centre of a volute: a Pietà; the Virgin seated, and holding the dead body of our Lord in her lap.

Pietà, in the British museum.

Statuettes in ivory were very numerous, and many beautiful examples are preserved in collections. Generally these represent the Virgin and Child; and are sometimes enclosed in canopied shrines, with the doors richly ornamented with carvings of subjects from the gospels. The robes were usually also coloured; and the woodcut, from an illumination in a French manuscript, shows a female artist at such work, with her palette, stool, and

An ivory painter at work.

brushes by her side. Modern taste runs rather against decoration of this kind, and denies that sculpture gains an improved effect by means of colour. But we must remember that colour was used at the best period of the Greek school, and the most famous statues which the world ever saw were thus ornamented over and above the use of a variety of material; such as gold and ivory together. Nor must we forget that we owe much of our knowledge of the details of dress, armour, and jewellery to the careful colouring of mediæval figures on tombs and monuments. Future generations may perhaps, not unreasonably, complain that we have left so few evidences of the decorations of our own time in imperishable materials like marble or bronze, or even in ivory.

Horns would be among the first things made from the tusks of elephants; the shape alone suggests its application to that purpose. Many very fine examples still exist; particularly what are known as tenure horns. The woodcut is engraved from a

Horn, fifteenth century.

horn of the 15th century, one of the most beautiful in any collection and now at South Kensington.

The next woodcut represents one line of six compartments,

Panels in open work.

Half of a diptych, English, in the British museum.

the same size as the original, from a book cover in the British museum. The whole cover is carved in open work of extreme delicacy, having altogether thirty such compartments; most of them filled with subjects from the gospels. This exquisite carving is probably French, of about the year 1350.

It is very difficult to determine the particular country in which many of the mediæval ivories were carved. It has long been the custom hastily to set down almost every ivory of the thirteenth and fourteenth centuries as Flemish or French, leaving but few except Italian marriage caskets to the credit of other countries. But, not to speak of Germany, there can be no question that carvings in ivory were much sought after and bought in England, and that there must have been numerous English artists. Two unquestionable examples of English ivories are in the British museum; and others are at South Kensington. The Ashmolean collection at Oxford possesses about a dozen ivory carvings almost all of which are of English workmanship. We may observe that commonly a peculiar *nez retroussé,* a smiling mouth, a general *gentillesse* of treatment, and a brilliant yet rapid mode of execution, stamp the French work with an almost unmistakable character. To the English style may be assigned a position midway between the French and the second Italian manner. It does not exhibit the gaiety and tenderness of the former, nor has it quite the grandeur of the latter, but is marked by a sober earnestness of expression in serious action which neither of those styles possesses. We may further remark that the English school had less of the monotony and mannerism which are the derogatory features of continental examples of the same period; in fact, English gothic ivories have both a purity and variety of treatment on a par with the admirable characteristics of contemporary architecture in this country.

Very few Spanish ivories of the middle ages can be referred to, and they generally have a very distinct Moorish or Persian character about them. They are almost all caskets or small boxes, and some are still to be found in the treasuries of churches in Spain. Two or three are at South Kensington, particularly a round box in open work with an Arabic inscription. Some of the Spanish ivories are as old as the days of the Cordovan caliphs in the ninth and tenth centuries. But unless there is an inscription we have scarcely any guide to direct us as to the date. Moorish art, like the Chinese, changed but little from age to age; the old process and the old patterns were handed down, unaltered, from father to son: and ivory carvings may have been made by Moorish workmen as late even as the year 1600.

The student will observe that more ivories in the great English collections—at Kensington, in the British museum, and at Liverpool—are attributed to the fourteenth century than to any other: this is equally true of collections abroad. Sculpture in ivory was especially and largely patronised at that time; and, with the exception of a very few examples of Roman art under the emperors, there are no carvings existing which equal those made from about the year 1280 to 1350, either in truth or gracefulness of design or in excellence of workmanship.

In the sixteenth and following centuries ivory carvers still produced many works, but in a style in which the influence of Italian and German artists became more and more perceptible. Some very minute carvings were also made in boxwood, and medallion portraits were also much in fashion. The artists of the renaissance sculptured with wonderful skill vases, sword handles, powder flasks, and other objects, decorated with arabesques, flowers and fruit, or groups of men and animals, or dancing boys. The best known of these was François du Quesnoy, or Il Fiammingo, whose works are of the highest quality. Nothing can surpass the grace and spirit of design in six plaques by Fiammingo in the Kensington collection, nor the excellence of the execution.

Another admirable example is a cylindrical goblet at Windsor castle. The bacchanalian figures upon this, especially the figures and children, display the utmost perfection of execution and power of rendering the appearance of a soft fleshy surface. Other artists, whose names are recorded, followed in the same style, and chiefly in producing large cups, cut from the thick part of tusks and covered with bas-reliefs from drawings after Rubens or Jordaens or German painters of the day.

Indian ivory comb.

Of oriental carvings in ivory little need be said; they are too well known to call for any description or account. The most intricate, and for patient workmanship the most wonderful, are the Chinese: Indian workmanship is more rude and coarse. On the other hand, the Japanese carvings are admirable for truthfulness and artistic spirit: more especially the small groups, or single figures, both of men and animals. All these are eminently characteristic of the particular country from whence they come; no one scarcely can mistake in distinguishing between ivories from China and Japan, or between the East Indian and Siamese and Persian. The same type and character continue also unchanged in each from century to century; as in Greece at the present time, where we find not only ivory carvings but other works retaining, unaltered, the symbolism and the style of Byzantine artists of a thousand years ago.

A word of caution will not be out of place with reference to the forgery of ivories. The great value of fine and early pieces has naturally led to imitations which are sometimes so well executed as to deceive people of much experience. A remarkable case occurred about ten years since in Belgium, where the government purchased a diptych, said to be of the consul Anastasius: £800 was given for it. A very learned Englishman, whose opinion was asked, expressed grave doubts as to the genuineness of the leaves; and further examination proved that his suspicions were well founded, and the diptych a modern forgery. The Belgian government brought an action against the dealer from whom it had been bought, and after some delay the money paid for it was recovered.

Much about the same time there were four or five important-looking ivories in the hands of some London dealers; one was a triptych, another a diptych, a third a comb, and a fourth was a huge shrine with folding shutters and richly decorated canopy, covering a statuette of the Virgin and Child. The forgery was in some respects successful; but in every piece there was a distinct character—the same in all—which proved their falseness. The great shrine, having been sold to an English collector for £500, was returned; but not long after was still to be seen for sale in a shop-window in the Strand, and said to be

116   *IVORIES.*

(as if to make confusion worse confounded) an ivory of the tenth century. Several of these pieces were traced back to a dealer at Amiens, and it is not now known what has become of any of them.

Two groups of the chessmen found in the island of Lewis.

POTTERY AND PORCELAIN.

Palissy dish: Kensington museum.

(M.F.A.)

POTTERY AND PORCELAIN.

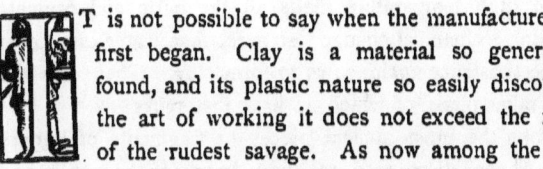IT is not possible to say when the manufacture of pottery first began. Clay is a material so generally to be found, and its plastic nature so easily discovered, that the art of working it does not exceed the intelligence of the rudest savage. As now among the most barbarous tribes earthenware utensils of various kinds are commonly in use, so we find at least fragments of pottery in the graves and ruined habitations of prehistoric people.

The first attempts to make vessels which would hold liquids reached no further than to those which could be made sufficiently hard by exposure to the sun. Such objects of sun-dried clay would be of a very perishable nature and could scarcely, except in the most dry climates, survive through a single winter. Egypt, Assyria, and Babylonia have transmitted to our days many sun-dried examples which represent very early efforts of the art. The baking of the clay, so as to produce an indestructible tenacity, must have been an immense stride; and was probably discovered by accident rather than design.

Although sun-dried vessels may be made of clay alone, yet in baking it undergoes a great alteration on account of its contractility by heat, and some siliceous substance incapable of contraction must enter into the body of the pottery. If we take a mere lump of clay soaked in water sufficiently to render it plastic, and fashion it into a bowl or brick and lay it in the sun to dry, the object hardens as the moisture evaporates and the particles adhere slightly together. We have thus obtained, however, only a brick or vessel of desiccated clay which may be again converted into its original state, by adding the lost quantity of water. But if the object be placed in a kiln, the nature of the clay is completely altered; the high temperature melts all the parts and cements them, effecting a chemical change; so great that water can never mix with the substance again, so as to form clay. Then also the contraction takes place, of which we have just spoken.

Even among the most ancient pieces or fragments of pottery which have been discovered we find specimens roughly and rudely ornamented. Whilst the clay was soft it was easy and natural to make marks and lines upon it, at first with the finger, afterwards with the finer point of the nail or a piece of horn or wood. As time went on, and men spread over the earth and assembled into tribes or nations, peculiar methods of mixing the clays and conventional forms and ornaments would be manifested by each. These have enabled us in modern days to trace many of the primitive vessels to their source, and appropriate them to their true makers with some degree of certainty.

We know that bricks were made in Egypt from the very earliest period of her history: and being often impressed with hieroglyphs they have served as historical records and have transmitted to us the names of a series of kings. Somewhat later, among the Assyrians little tablets and cylinders of terra cotta were employed for writing upon, and were used for their public archives, their operations of trade, and historical annals. Some of these cylinders and other relics, still extant, contain the history of Tiglath Pileser and the campaign of Sennacherib against the Jews. To this indestructible material we are indebted for a detailed account of many important facts in the Assyrian history; whilst some of the decades of Livy and the plays of Menander, written upon more perishable stuff, have been wholly lost.

The potter's wheel was an early invention and a vast improvement upon the methods previously adopted in fashioning the sun-dried clay by the hand alone. These could have produced only vessels of a very rude and unsymmetrical shape. But the application of a circular table or lathe, laid horizontally and revolving on a central pivot, on which the clay was placed and to which it adhered, was a truly wonderful advance in the art. As the wheel spun round all combinations of oval, spherical, and cylindrical forms could be arrived at, and vases became not merely symmetrical in their proportions but true in their capacity.

The invention of the wheel has been ascribed to all the great nations of antiquity. It is represented in the Egyptian sculptures, it is mentioned in the Scriptures, and was in use from a remote period in Assyria. The oldest vases of Greece, some of which have been attributed to the heroic ages, bear marks of having been turned upon the wheel.

Greek vase, signed by Nicosthenes.

The next step was to render the clay vessels less porous and better fitted to hold liquids by covering them with an impervious glaze. Opaque glasses or enamels as old as the time of Moses have been found in Egypt. The employment of copper to obtain a brilliant blue enamel was very early both in Assyria and Babylonia; and the use of tin for a white enamel, as recently found in the enamelled bricks and vases of those ancient countries, anticipated by many centuries the rediscovery of that process in Europe in the fifteenth century and shows the early application of metallic oxides.

Pottery is either soft or hard. The terms have reference to the composition as well as to the degree of heat to which it is exposed in the furnace. Thus, common brick is soft; fire-brick hard. Common earthenware vessels are soft; crockery, such as stone ware, is hard. Porcelain is also distinguished by the technical terms "soft" and " hard paste," the softness being determined by the greater proportion of silex.

Porcelain is composed of two substances; the one fusible which produces its transparency, the other infusible. The best practical test to distinguish the two descriptions is that the body of the soft paste can be scratched with a knife, which is not the case with hard paste. The ancient pottery of Egypt, Greece, and Rome was soft; whether glazed, unglazed, or lustrous. In our own days oriental porcelain may be taken as a type of hard, and early Sèvres or Chelsea of soft paste manufacture.

The body of hard porcelain is formed of "kaolin;" which is a natural decomposition of granite. Used alone kaolin would be opaque; but by the mixture of a perfectly transparent and highly refractive substance it is rendered capable of transmitting light, as paper is made translucent with oil. This refractive agent is "petunse" or china-stone; containing much unchanged felspar, which also supplies the principal material for the glaze.

Examples of Egyptian pottery are to be found in most of the great collections and in national museums. Pottery was not only an important branch of the domestic arts of Egypt, but was largely employed for making vases to hold portions of the dead bodies which were to be embalmed. For daily use they had vessels of various shapes and sizes; some as large as several feet high; some scarcely an inch. These were used not alone for liquids but for bread and meat, for ointments, drugs, and sweetmeats. Besides existing specimens which have been found in tombs, paintings have been discovered showing the potters at their work. A scene upon a wall at Beni Hassan represents the kneading of the clay, rolling out the paste, placing it on the wheel and fashioning it with the hands. The Egyptians knew also how to make a ware which appears to correspond with modern porcelain. Strictly this was not porcelain, not being translucent nor so compact. The colours, green, red, yellow, or violet, are all good; but the best was a fine celestial blue, probably obtained from an oxide of copper, which has been scarcely rivalled after three thousand years of later human experience. Amulets, rings, little vases, the decorations of mummy cases, bottles, beads, and the like, were made of this material. Of a larger size, the chief objects were sepulchral figures, covered with hieroglyphs, to be placed in the tombs.

We have already spoken of the cylinders and tablets used for writing on by the Assyrians; and everywhere in the ruins of Babylonia fragments of glazed ware have been found. The most numerous and the least imperfect are the coffins made of this kind of ware. They are shaped like a slipper with a large oval aperture above, through which the body was introduced and then closed in with a lid of earthenware.

A few vases and large quantities of broken pieces of earthen vessels have been found on the sites of some of the cities of Judæa; at Jerusalem, Bethlehem, and elsewhere. The Hebrew potters do not seem to have been distinguished in the art, and there are comparatively few notices of it in the scriptures; but there was a guild of potters at Jerusalem and one of the gates of the city was named after them.

Passing from these old oriental nations we find the greatest excellence among the Greeks. The beauty and simplicity of the forms of their vases have caused them to be regarded as models; and by the addition of painting they have become an almost inexhaustible source for illustrating the mythology, the history, and the customs of the people.

The term now commonly in use for the potter's art, namely, ceramic or keramic, is from the Greek *Keramos*, supposed to have been derived from *Keras*, a horn, probably the primitive material from which drinking vessels were made.

The use of terra cotta among the Greeks was very extensive. It was employed in buildings for roof and drain tiles, columns, and other architectural members. Statues were made of it for the temples, small decorations of various kinds for personal wear, and ornaments for houses; besides, of course, vases and culinary and domestic utensils, and lamps. Numerous examples of all these classes may be seen in most of the great national collections at home and abroad: the chief of them and the most beautiful are the vases.

Terra cotta (as its name imports) is simply baked clay; but much skill and care are necessary in its composition, so as to ensure the right degree of hardness. The principal material is common potter's clay, with which a certain quantity of broken earthenware is mixed: these being finely kneaded together are moulded into the required forms, which are placed in the kiln. When properly burnt, terra cotta is harder and more endurable than natural stones.

The terra cotta vases of the ancients are of various shapes; and many of them, intended for ornamental purposes, are covered with a white coating and painted with colours; a few simple ornaments, or plain bands, or chequered wreaths. But there was another kind of vase, made of a paste composed of a substance very similar to terra cotta, yet deeper in tone and more tender in its texture. This last, however, varies; being sometimes so hard as scarcely to admit of a cut with a knife; sometimes so soft as to be easily scratched with a finger-nail. These vases show, at their best period, the highest point of perfection which the ancient potteries attained. They are painted with various colours, chiefly black, brown, yellow and red, covered with a thin alkaline glaze, which is transparent and enhances the colours like the varnish of a picture. They are so porous that water will ooze through them, and the paste when struck gives a dull metallic sound.

Vases of this description have been found not only in Greece but in such large quantities in Etruria that the name Etruscan has been long and very commonly given to them. The discoveries in

Etruria and Campania are the work of Greek artists, and the style of painting as well as the designs completely Greek. The Etruscans were accustomed to inscribe their own art productions with the peculiar characters of the nation; but it is believed that no good painted vase has yet been found with any other than a Greek inscription. The number of vases which have been found—it need scarcely be said, all, with very few exceptions, in the old graves and larger tombs — seems incredible: probably the total in public and private collections exceeds 40,000. There are about 5000 in the British museum, 1500 at Paris, and nearly 2000 at Berlin.

Etruscan vase.

We have no means of ascertaining the date of the oldest glazed vases without inscriptions. Some may reach as far back as nine or ten centuries before our æra, and they come down to as late a period as the second century after Christ. More than one attempt has been made to classify them, but all are somewhat arbitrary.

Very briefly it may be said that the archaic period ended about 700 B.C. and many of the first examples were made with the hand. They are rude also in the painted decorations. For a century or two the style of art continued to be severe, but with increasing skill both in design and execution. The figures are in black on a red ground, and the outlines usually engraved with a point; the subjects being heroic and mythological. The best period succeeded, and extends from the sixth to the fourth century before Christ.

In looking at the admirable productions of this age we must

remember that the drawings were executed upon the moist clay, so that great freedom of touch and unhesitating decision were required; for no mark once made could be obliterated, and a complete and perfect line was to be traced without taking the brush from the surface. The vases were painted in an upright position, and the eye of the artist was his only guide. Notwithstanding all the difficulties the ancients observed the laws of equilibrium in their figures; conveyed expression by means of attitude; and by the use of profile and the introduction of small objects into the background compensated for the want of perspective.

The instruments employed by the Greek potters must have been like those in use at the present day. The apparent fineness of the exterior is solely due to the care with which the surface was polished. The paintings were made with a kind of brush, a stick being used to steady the hand. The outlines were formed with a pointed tool, and the incised circular lines in shields apparently with a compass.

From the fourth century B.C. to the second of the Christian æra a gradual decline is to be traced in the Greek vases; to be observed in an exaggeration of the proportions and in superabundance of ornamentation. About the year 200 the making of them altogether ceased.

From the very earliest times the island of Samos was renowned for its fictile ware; and the oldest description of the potter's art in literature is in one of the Homeric hymns addressed to the Samian potters. This ware—the famous so called Samian ware—retained its renown till the days

Fragment of Samian ware, found in France.

of the Roman empire : and evidence of Roman occupation
may almost always be shown in excavations by the discovery
of some fragments. The most remarkable fact connected with
this ware is not only its uniform density and texture but its
colour, a beautiful coralline red. As it is difficult to comprehend how this should be the same everywhere—whether in
Germany, France, or England,—however distant the localities
may be and the difference of soil in each, we can but refer to
one district as the place of its manufacture : or, at any rate,
from whence the clay was supplied for making it in some few
Roman towns in western Europe. We know, moreover, that
Pliny expressly says that the Samian ware was exported not
only to Rome but "to every nation under heaven."

The general forms of the Samian ware are bowls and dishes
of considerable thickness, as if intended to bear constant wear
and frequent removal. The ornamentation is peculiar and cha-

Samian bowl.

racteristic; moulded in relief upon the exterior, the interior
having been first rounded smoothly into a perfect form by the
lathe. Some of the patterns are beautiful; and a few among
them are valuable as illustrating gladiatorial combats and Roman
games and customs. The scrolls, most usual as an ornament,
are exceedingly elegant; generally varieties of the tendrils,
flowers, leaves, and fruit of the ivy or the vine. Repetition
was greatly sought; and, as in the general decline of any

art, the ornaments occupy much space in proportion to the surface.

Very numerous examples of Roman pottery (and their potteries were spread everywhere) are to be studied in museums; chiefly, urns and lamps, culinary vessels, cups for drinking, and large amphoræ. The lamps are beautifully decorated with elaborate subjects in relief: from the fables of Æsop, the legends of Rome, or love-scenes and the like. One of the finest is in the British musuem; a race of four-horsed chariots, in the amphitheatre: and another, very remarkable; in which the bowl has in relief a copy of the seven-branched golden candlestick of the temple of Jerusalem.

Ancient Gallic vase.

In excavations and in graves in most of the northern and western countries of Europe fragments of very ancient pottery often occur; and not seldom also complete pieces. It is not necessary to do much more than refer to the fact. The vases of the Stone period found in tumuli are generally of an urn shape with wide open mouths, and tapering at the feet. They are so friable that they could scarcely have been made for domestic use but, probably, for sepulchral rites. The ornament is of the simplest kind; cords or bands;

Ancient British bowl.

and made with coarse instruments. They are not turned with the wheel but fashioned by the hand. So, also, in much later ages, down to the British and Romano-British times, we find only a gradual, and very slow and slight, improvement. In short, the

POTTERY AND PORCELAIN. 129

early pottery of the nations which inhabited northern and western Europe was of the lowest order with respect to those qualities which we esteem in the potter's art.

With the fall of the Roman empire all the arts declined; and some of them to so great an extent that for a long time they may be said to have been almost extinct. Probably no branch suffered so much as the art of pottery. The process of the

Mediæval jars and basin.

lustrous glazing seems to have been lost before the third century began, and we may say that for a thousand years we have no examples left—with one exception—which we might call artistic. That exception, the Hispano-moresque, will be spoken of more fully in another section, on Maiolica.

When Theophilus wrote in the 12th century, and explained the various industries of the nations of Europe, he mentions only the pottery of the Greeks. He speaks of a process which they used to decorate their pottery, by means of vitrifiable colours

9

(true enamels) and with gold and silver applied with the brush. But we know nothing of the nature of the clay, nor whether it

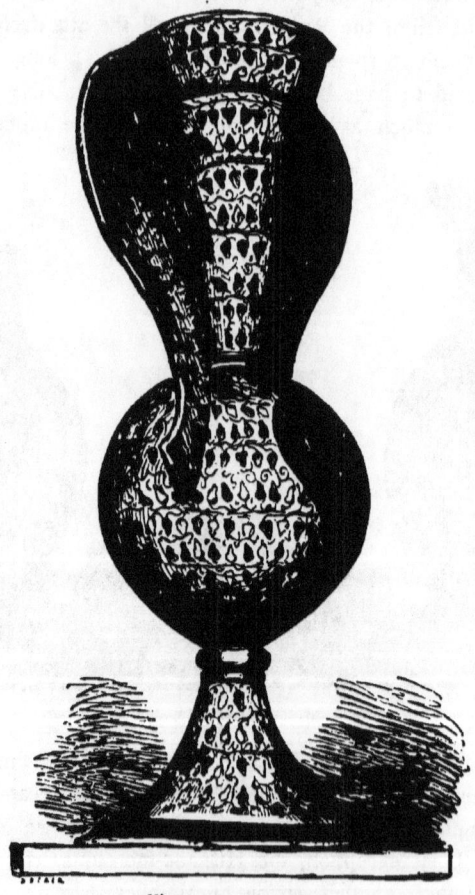

Hispano-moresque vase.

was glazed. Neither is there, we believe, in any museum or collection a single specimen which can be referred to. We must not, however, omit to notice that some very admirable busts and statuettes were executed in the north of Italy about the middle of the fifteenth century.

Terra cotta; Florentine; fifteenth century.

In France many towns became well known as centres of the manufacture of pottery, about the beginning of the fifteenth century. In inventories of that date specimens are described of

Pilgrim's bottle; Nevers.

Beauvais ware, which were so highly esteemed as to be mounted in silver. It is necessary to name only one other place, Nevers, where enamelled pottery was first made in France under the patronage of Catherine of Medicis. This manufactory has continued down to the present time. The Nevers ware of the best period (the beginning of the seventeenth century) is very beautiful, and there is a large collection in the museum of that town. Although sometimes an imitation of the Italian mai-

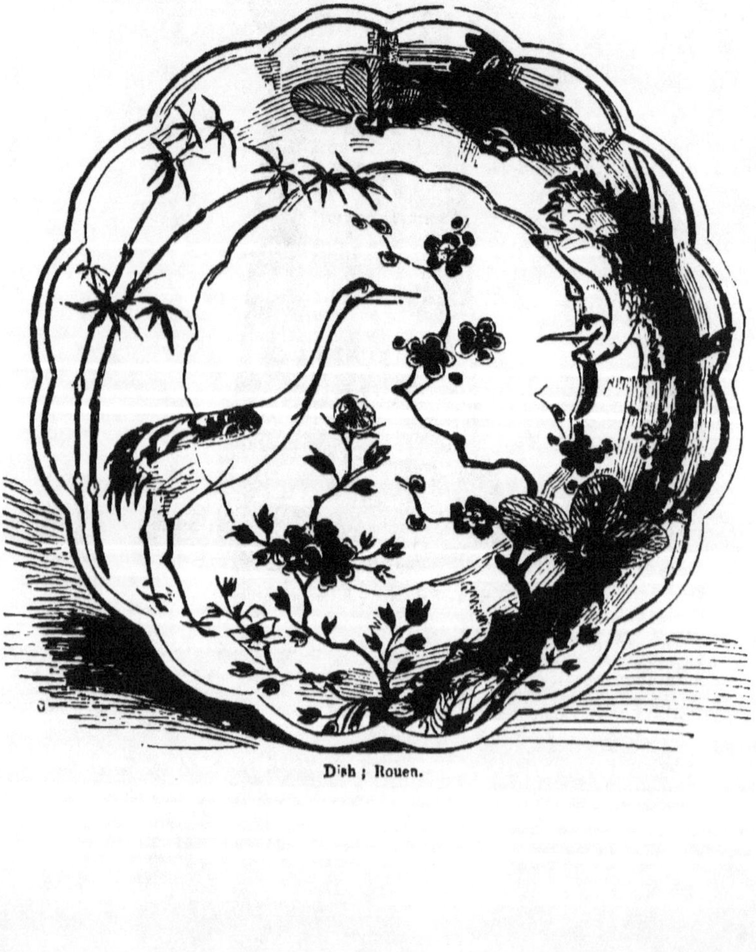

Dish; Rouen.

olica it yet differs from this in many respects. The outlines of the figures in such specimens are traced in violet, the flesh is yellow : a copper-green is a peculiarity, and red is seldom used. Blue and yellow are the predominating colours, separated by a line of white. About the same period, good pieces were also made at Rouen. These are sometimes of a large size, fountains, vases, busts, etc., and are of a later date. Moustiers, in

Rouen vase.

the south of France, also produced some fine pottery, and succeeded in reaching a high degree of refinement. Examples are very rare.

The two most famous wares of France, of the time of the renaissance, are the Palissy and the Henri Deux. Bernard Palissy was born about 1510, of poor parents, who could give him but little education. He learned to read and write, and

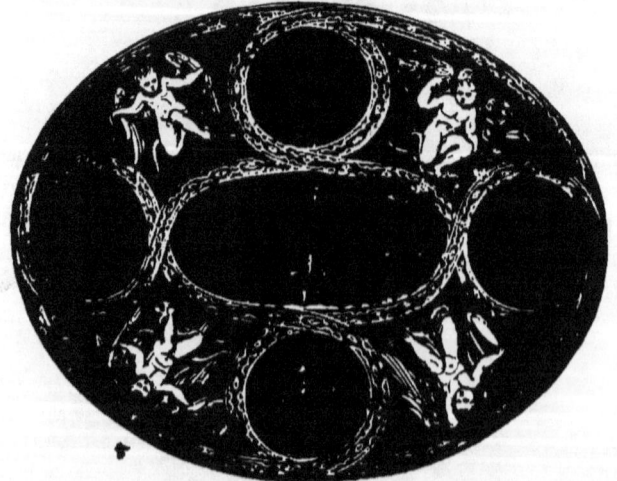

Moustiers dish.

Palissy dish: Kensington museum.

taught himself geometry, drawing, and modelling. Beginning as a workman in glass, having made himself master of that business, he travelled and studied natural history and chemistry. A few years after his marriage in 1539 he saw a cup of enamelled pottery, and it struck him that if he could discover the com-

Salt cellar; Palissy: Kensington museum.

position of the enamel he would raise the art of pottery to an eminence hitherto unknown and secure his own fortune. He knew nothing of the process or of the materials: but he made experiment after experiment, and spent all his money in useless attempts. He has described, in his own book, his labours, his trials and disappointments. He would yield to no complaints of his wife or the arguments of friends; once, when no more money could be borrowed, he burned the tables and boards of his house for fuel to supply his furnace. At length he was successful: he discovered the secret of the enamel, and his pottery soon obtained him wealth and fame.

The fayence of Palissy is characterised by a peculiar style and many peculiar qualities. It is not decorated with flat painting. His figures and his ornaments are all executed in coloured relief. The back of his pieces is never of an uniform colour, but mottled with blue, yellow, and brown. The natural objects which he modelled are very true in form and colour: he

136   POTTERY AND PORCELAIN.

Palissy fruit plate.

placed upon his dishes fish, reptiles, and plants carefully formed,

Reptile dish; Palissy.

probably, from living specimens. Sometimes fossil shells, so correctly that their species can be recognised. These "rustic

Palissy cup with shells.

pieces," as he himself named them, were not made for use but only for ornament. He made also vases with elaborate decorations, salt-cellars, inkstands, dishes, ewers and statuettes. It is right to

Palissy dish.

say that some doubt exists as to the statuettes : and the famous "Nurse" and the "Girl with the puppies" are possibly by some other hand. The costumes seem to be a little later than Palissy's time.

Palissy mould.

Some few years ago, in digging a trench in Paris, traces of the workshop of Palissy were discovered; with fragments of his pottery and some moulds intended to be used : these are in high relief, portions of the human figure.

Imitations of Palissy's work were made after his death ; those attempted in modern days can rarely be mistaken for the true ware: they are overloaded with ornament. Even under his immediate successors, some perhaps who had worked under him, the art greatly deteriorated. The talent and the taste of the inventor disappeared; and we have monotonous repetitions. The care displayed in the manufacture of the true pieces, the sharpness of the relievo decorations, the purity of the tint, and the brilliancy of the enamel colours, are tests by which they may be distinguished from later productions of the same kind. Very large collections of Palissy ware and admirable examples are in the Paris museums and at Sèvres: there are good specimens also in the British museum and at South Kensington.

Genuine pieces of Palissy ware have become very rare;

naturally it would be so, when so many have been procured for and are shut up in national collections. At the Pourtalès sale in 1865, a reptile dish sold for £28; a recumbent female for £112; another dish, £40; and a square salt-cellar for £202.

The so-called Henri Deux ware, now more properly described as Oiron ware, is unique of its kind: and until lately nothing was known with certainty either as to its producer or the place of its origin. Some have thought it to be Italian work: but it differs too essentially from the Italian maiolica to admit of this conjecture. No specimen has yet been found in that country: and the majority of the pieces have been brought from Touraine and La Vendée. Within the last few years, a large amount of evidence has been brought forward, we may almost say conclusive, that they were made at Oiron in Poitou. We have sufficient evidence as to the date of the manufacture. Upon some of the earlier pieces are emblems of Francis the first; and on a greater number we see the device of Henry the second with the crescents interlaced, said to refer to Diana of Poitiers.

The paste used for modelling this ware is a true pipeclay, fine and very white; so that it does not require, like the Italian fayence, to be concealed by a coating of opaque enamel: the decorations are merely glazed with a very thin varnish, yellowish, and transparent. These decorations consist of initial letters, interlacings, and arabesques impressed upon the paste, and the

Ewer; Oiron ware.

cavities filled in with coloured pastes, so as to present a smooth surface of the finest inlaying, like the damascening of metal work. The ornaments, which are drawn with wonderful clearness and precision, are not traced with a brush (as might be at first sight supposed) but are engraved in the paste, and the colouring substances have been then incrusted in the depressions so as to leave no inequalities upon the surface. After the completion of this operation the object was baked and then glazed. These (as it were) inlaid ornaments appear to have been produced by the tools used by bookbinders, or even in some cases by stamps; and the patterns undoubtedly bear a resemblance to the book-binding of Grolier and Maioli.

Candlestick; Oirou ware.

In addition to these elegant niello-like decorations, the Oiron ware is enriched with raised ornaments in bold relief; masks, escutcheons, shells, wreaths, etc. The forms are always pure in outline and in the style of the renaissance; so that this exquisite pottery may be justly compared with the chased and damascened metal work of the sixteenth century.

The very high money value of this admirable class of earthenware has arisen from several causes; but especially from its intrinsic artistic merit. Whilst displaying great variety in their forms and details the pieces are all conceived in the same general style, typical of a well-known and brilliant epoch, and in the highest degree personal and local. In fact, there can be no doubt that this famous pottery, as is the case with the Palissy ware, was the work or conception of one artist; perhaps by the hand, certainly under the patronage, of a woman, Héléne de Hangest-Genlis.

Oiron pottery.

At present about eighty pieces of Oiron or Henri Deux ware are supposed to exist; and none is a duplicate of another. Five of these, a salver, a candlestick, a salt-cellar, and two tazzas are in the South Kensington museum. No other public collection in England can boast of one. Two are in the museum of the Louvre and one at the hôtel Cluny. The five pieces at South Kensington cost more than £1800; they would probably fetch now, if they could be sold, double the money. A "biberon" or drinking cup at a sale in Paris in 1865 was sold for £1100; and a small salt-cellar was bought privately about the same time for £700.

The celebrated productions of Sèvres are porcelain, not pottery. Other places had preceded Sèvres in the manufacture, especially St. Cloud: and about the year 1670 various attempts were made in France to imitate the Indian porcelain. The paste of the porcelain of St. Cloud is compact and milky in colour and the lead glaze vitreous and unequally laid on, so as to be apt to settle into drops. The decorations are often birds and flowers in relief, like the white oriental.

Very marvellous works in porcelain, especially flowers and bouquets, were made early in the seventeenth century at Vincennes; under the patronage of Louis the fifteenth. Once, when the king visited madame de Pompadour she took him into a hothouse where was a parterre, filled with roses, lilies and other flowers, and of delicate perfume. The king stooped to gather one, and had scarcely touched it before he discovered that they were Vincennes porcelain scented with volatilised essences.

Old Sèvres porcelain of the "pâte tendre" or soft body, is unquestionably the most beautiful and precious porcelain ever produced. The earliest dated specimen is 1753: and the manufacture of the true and highest quality (the soft paste) was discontinued about the year 1800 from various causes, the principal of which was doubtless the then general decline of taste in matters of art. The "pâte tendre" porcelain of Sèvres is a purely chemical composition, very soft and vitreous, and can be entirely welled in the furnace at very high temperature, but the hard porcelain cannot. The superadded glaze which covers it is also richer in texture than that of the inferior quality: it incorporates to a certain extent with the body, forming a more homogeneous and beautiful surface, and the enamel colours painted on it blend with it and assume the most lustrous hues. The painted decorations, indeed, of the old " pâte tendre" have an impasto like the best oil painting, and a depth and smoothness of tone, easily appreciable.

The more modern hard porcelain of Sèvres, even the splendid ware of the present day, is distinguished by very different qualities, and a slight examination shows its inferiority. Hard paste in comparison with soft has a crude and faded look ; and the enamel colours rest upon the surface instead of mingling with or sinking into it.

Sèvres porcelain for domestic use had commonly a plain ground, painted with flowers detached or in wreaths. Pieces intended for decoration or for state dinner services had generally coloured grounds, such as the "bleu de roi" or "blue turquoise," or green, or especially the lovely rose pink to which the name of Dubarry is usually attached ; although the colour had been invented some years before her appearance at court. Very skilful artists were employed upon the highest class, which is decorated with landscapes, flowers, birds and cupids, gracefully disposed in medallions of every variety of beautiful form. The portraits and miniatures are of a later date. Nor must we omit

Sèvres vase; bleu de roi.

to notice the jewelled cups of the best time; which, if genuine, are upon the bleu de roi ground. Sèvres produced also admirably modelled groups and single figures in biscuit, the models for which were supplied by Falconnet; one of the most famous is " the bather."

Sèvres porcelain has always been an extremely expensive production, and the cost of the pieces when first made bore a nearer proportion to their value, until within the last few years, than is generally supposed. The finest examples were made expressly for royalty or sold (by permission) for large sums. But lately the prices given for the rarest specimens, especially for sets of vases, has been increasing and seems to be enormous. In 1850 cups and saucers were thought to be extravagantly bought for £25 or £30 a piece; or bowls and dishes, for £60 or £70; or, again, when three oviform vases and covers, in Lord Pembroke's sale, fetched £1020. But at Mr. Bernal's sale a pair of rose Dubarry vases were sold for 1850 guineas; and cups and saucers for £100. The prices, however, still increased; and single plates have since been sold for £200, vases for 500 or 600 guineas each; and cups and saucers for 150 guineas. Can we say that the extreme has yet been arrived at, when we remember that a year ago a set of three jardinières fetched at Christie's, by auction, the enormous sum of £10,000?

With regard to the marks on Sèvres porcelain, all pieces are considered to have been painted before 1753 which have the crossed L s without a letter. At that date a letter of the alphabet, marking each year and beginning with A, was placed between the interlacing L s: thus, 1753 is indicated by A, and Z is reached in 1776. The following year is marked with a double A.

After the general introduction of Chinese porcelain into Europe by the Portuguese, chemists for two centuries endeavoured to imitate it, but could make no nearer approach than earthenware. The first European hard porcelain was made at Dresden by Böttcher, after numberless experiments and years of labour; and

POTTERY AND PORCELAIN.

the first manufactory was established at Weissen in 1715, under the patronage of Augustus II, elector of Saxony. Böttcher was appointed the director.

The earliest Böttcher ware is reddish brown and unglazed; stone ware rather than porcelain, and his first white porcelain pieces were ornamented with flowers in low relief. Unwearied as his efforts had been, chance and not science at last brought him the material which he wanted. A white soft earth had been introduced, ground into an impalpable dust, as a substitute for wheat flower for hair powder at that time in general use. Böttcher observed one day its unusual weight and inquired where the powder came from. He learned that it was earthy; he tried it; and found it to be the long sought for " kaolin," the substance which forms the principal basis of porcelain.

Improvements rapidly grew in the manufacture of Dresden china. At first the subjects painted were imitations of Chinese decoration; but these were soon succeeded by magnificent services with intricate gold borders, and medallions with flowers and other designs. Then followed vases and other objects with exquisite paintings upon richly coloured grounds, copies of the best pictures of the Flemish school, or birds and insects, flowers and animals. Modelled flowers and little statuettes, candlesticks, groups and single figures, are also among the most beautiful productions of

Dresden candelabrum.

the best period of Dresden china The quality greatly declined towards the end of the eighteenth century. The well-known Dresden mark, the crossed swords, was first used about the year 1722.

Dresden was not the only German city which became famous in the last century for porcelain: at Vienna, Berlin, Frankenthal, Furstenburg, and other places were very celebrated manufactories, but our space will not permit any separate account of them. The different qualities and marks are explained in many of the large works upon pottery.

Delft, a town between the Hague and Rotterdam, was celebrated for its wares at a very early period; which seem to have been imported into England as far back as the reign of Henry the fourth; and some "immense Delft ware dishes" were given by Philip of Austria, governor of the Netherlands, to Sir Thomas Trenchard in 1506. The principal centres of the manufacture of this kind of pottery were Delft and Haarlem. Of all fayence (before Wedgwood) delft has the thinnest and the lightest paste, as thin sometimes as the finest oriental and very sonorous. The potters of Rouen never painted figures in landscapes, but the ware of Holland was decorated by its best painters. A large proportion of delft was copied from the old Japan porcelain, both in form and colour. The three ringed bottles, the shapeless beaker, and the large circular dish are to be seen in most collections; and they well imitate both the pattern and the colour of the originals. This imitation oriental ware was covered with a bluish glaze or enamel, presenting a smooth surface. Marl or sand was mixed with the clay, in order to lessen the contraction in baking, giving

Delft vase.

also a lightness and hardness which had not been attained in any other manufacture.

The making of oriental looking delft was introduced into England by Dutch potters. Bristol, Lambeth, and Fulham appear to have been the sites of the potteries.

Stoneware, of ancient origin in the east, was probably first made in Europe in Germany, at Ratisbon, Cologne, and other places. It is a dense and highly vitrified earthenware, impervious

German ware; sixteenth century.

to the action of acids, and is formed of clay mixed with sand. The glazing is the actual material itself fused together, with the addition of salt thrown into the kiln. When broken it exhibits a close grey texture, is impermeable to liquid and resists the action of fire. It is of extraordinary hardness and will strike fire with steel.

The brown stone pots known as greybeards were made in

great numbers, and exported to England and various countries. Another extensive class is designated as "Grès de Flandre;" but somewhat wrongly as it was rarely, if ever, made in Flanders but in some of the towns in Germany. Another class is remarkable for its beautiful blue colour, its quaint forms and rich ornaments. Very fine specimens of these different divisions are to be found in most of the national collections.

We come now to England, and have already spoken of the more ancient and ruder kinds; and of the Samian ware, which has been found in almost every place which had been occupied by the Romans, in the first century of the Christian æra. The next earliest specimens of decorative fictile ware which we possess are the ornamental tiles with which the old churches and abbeys were paved. These were probably of English workmanship, and are generally of better make and with more artistic ornamentation than the tiles which have been found upon the continent. Sometimes, these tiles were made in moulds with the pattern in relief; and coated with an uniform green or brown glaze. Sometimes, with such patterns in outline and of the same colour as the tile. Sometimes, with the pattern inlaid. This last is the most common variety. After the pattern had been impressed the sunk portions were filled in with white clay, and the whole covered with yellow glaze, producing a bright yellow ornament on a rich brown ground. Four of the old kilns have been discovered; at Bawsey, near Lynn; near Droitwich; at Great Malvern; and at Great Saredon, in Staffordshire.

The manufacture of ornamental earthenware does not appear to have been extensively practised in England during the middle ages. Fragments of pottery have been frequently found; but examples of perfect pieces very rarely, and it is hardly possible to appropriate them to their particular date. These have been discovered chiefly in excavations in London; and we can scarcely speak of them as works of art, being of homely manufacture and for domestic use. A very curious jug or ewer was found at

Lewes, in 1845; of a date as early, perhaps, as the reign of Henry the second. Occasionally reference is made to certain

Green ewer; found at Lewes.

kinds of earthenware vessels in mediæval inventories, such as pitchers and pots and especially the "crusekyn." This last seems to have been the best kind, and was in some instances so valued as to be mounted in silver. The word is still in use in Ireland to denote a small pot or cup. The "greybeards" were largely imported; and in James the first's time commonly went by the name of "Bellarmins." Jugs in imitation of these greybeards were made in England as early as the reign of queen Elizabeth: and in 1626 letters patent were granted to certain London merchants for the sole making of "Stone pottes, stone jugges, and stone bottells, for the terme of fourteene yeares." The same document declares that up to that time such things had been brought "out of foreign partes, from beyond the seas." Earthenware jugs were also made in France, about the year 1600.

Earthenware jug; French.

Delft and stoneware were not uncommon in England long ago, though it is not known where the first manufactures were situated. The earliest specimens are of the reign of Charles the first; white jugs; or wine pots, marked for "sack," "claret," or "whit." Occasionally they have dates: ranging from 1642 to 1659. Delft potteries were carried on at Lambeth until comparatively a recent period. The earliest document to which we can refer relating to stoneware is a petition addressed to lord

Burghley, in 1581, as to establishing such a pottery in this country. The troubles in the Netherlands, which drove so many industrious workmen to other places, probably induced also makers of different kinds of pottery to settle here. Whether any (even of the last years of Elizabeth) of the beautiful though plainly mottled brown stoneware jugs, which are found mounted in silver, were made in England is very doubtful : the mountings are undeniably English, and often richly gilt and of admirable design and workmanship.

Staffordshire, in which is the large district called the Potteries, has been immemorially celebrated for its earthenware. Some have traced the manufacture, in the shape of tiles and jars and jugs, through the times of the Dane and the Saxon up to the Romans. Be this as it may, we have in a book of household accounts of the year 1466, an entry of a payment of four shillings and sixpence by Sir John Howard, to one of the potters of Horkesley, for eleven dozen pots. There are examples still extant as old as the reign of Elizabeth, and dishes with the arms and of the date of Charles the first.

The names of many manufacturers of about the end of the seventeenth century are on record ; the chief, perhaps, among them being that of two brothers, the Elers, from Nuremberg, who discovered near Bradwell a bed of fine compact red clay, which enabled them to imitate the red ware of Japan. For some years they kept the method of their process secret; but being discovered numerous establishments soon competed with them. The introduction of the salt glaze, one of the greatest improvements in the potter's art, is due to the Elers.

Josiah Wedgwood is the most widely celebrated of all English potters. When he began his career almost all objects of English origin for ornamenting mantelpieces and cabinets and window-sills were in a very rude state. Only rich people could afford to purchase Dresden or Chelsea china; and clumsily fashioned pots for flowers and coarsely modelled figures were the only decorations of rooms in middle-class houses. Wedgwood was born at Burslem, in 1730, of a family which had carried on the manufacture for some years. About the year 1755 he succeeded in discovering the green glaze which covers the well-known and still favourite dessert plates and dishes with imitation vineleaves and fruit. In 1762 he produced the fine cream-coloured ware which gained him great reputation and was called *Queen's ware.* This is composed of the finest clays from Devon and Dorset, mixed with a due proportion of ground flint. In 1768 he took out a patent for encaustic painting "in imitation of the ancient Etruscan earthenware," and in 1769 opened the new manufactory at Etruria. In 1773 another improvement was made, "a fine white terra cotta, proper for cameos, portraits, and bas-reliefs:" this was the forerunner of the beautiful jasper ware.

Vase; Wedgwood; blue jasper.

This last was among the most remarkable productions of Wedgwood. It is a white porcellaneous biscuit of exquisite delicacy which has the property of receiving through the whole substance, from the admixture of metallic oxides, the same colours as the oxides communicate to glass or enamels. It is admirably adapted for all subjects which should be shown in relief. The ground can be made of any colour, whilst the raised figures are of the purest white. The numbers which were made are astonishing; nearly 1000 are enumerated in Wedgwood's own catalogue, all (it is said) taken from original gems lent for the purpose. For other works such as plaques, or vases, Flaxman supplied many drawings and models. The most important and valuable piece of Wedgwood ware is the copy of the famous

Portland vase, originally sold for fifty guineas each; and for which much higher prices have since been given. An example is in the South Kensington museum.

Other well-known potteries in England were at Lambeth, as far back as 1640, and at Fulham a few years later. Fulham stoneware is of exceedingly hard texture, very compact and covered with a salt glaze: ornamented with a brilliant blue enamel in bands, leaves, and flowers, often with medallions also.

Earthenware seems to have been made at Bristol as early as the reign of Edward the first; and there was a manufactory there in the time of queen Elizabeth. So also at Leeds, Yarmouth, and Lowestoft. At the last place, pieces of oriental white porcelain seem to have been painted with Chinese designs; but it is incorrect to attribute, as some are disposed, every doubtful piece of a certain quality and decoration to Lowestoft.

Before we speak of English porcelain it would be well to make a few remarks upon oriental porcelain; of China and Japan. We are unable to decide at how far back a date oriental china may have been brought to Europe. It is quite possible that the Romans, under the empire, may have had many specimens: nor is there any extravagance in supposing that some of the famous vases, spoken of by late authors and in a material about which we are uncertain, may have been Chinese porcelain. Before the beginning of the sixteenth century we find several passages in travels and histories which speak of the beauty and excellence of oriental china. The earliest known pieces in England are some bowls given by Philip of Austria to Sir Thomas Trenchard in 1506, and still preserved in that family. These are blue and white Nankin. Another is a pale sea green basin, of thick ware, at New College, Oxford, said to have been archbishop Warham's, about 1520; and later, in queen Elizabeth's reign, we have mention made in various records of " porselyn " and " Chinese stuffe."

The period of the first manufacture of porcelain in China is involved in complete obscurity: we must be content to allow it a very great antiquity and admit that excellence was long ago arrived at. We cannot base any argument upon the little Chinese bottles found in the tombs of Egypt with remains of mummies, for these seem unquestionably to be of a much later time, and to have been fraudulently put there by the Arabs. On the other hand there appears no reason for disputing the official annals of the Chinese themselves, which have placed the invention some two hundred years at least before the Christian æra. The marvellously delicate and thin egg-shell vases, cups, and plates, appear to have been first made about the middle of the sixteenth century.

Many attempts have been made to classify the various kinds of Chinese porcelain; a task of extreme difficulty. The dragon, with five, four, or three claws, is a favourite subject of decoration; also, the kylin, the dog, the spotted deer, and sacred birds. The most beautiful colour is the turquoise blue; and really old examples are very rare; still more rare is the old violet. Yellow is the imperial colour; and a fine ruby is generally found on the highest quality of egg-shell plates. The old sea-green, the true céladon, is greatly valued and also rare. The crackle vases, when good and old, are always sought after: and though the cause of the crackles is shown to

Oriental (Chinese) vase.

be the unequal expansion of the glaze on the paste, we do not exactly know how they were produced.

The Chinese made wonderful porcelain : to which they gave innumerable forms and every gradation of colour. The decorative taste and skill of the artists of "the celestial empire" know no limits. Their chief aim was to imitate, with more or less capricious variation, some natural object. They studied flowers and fruits, beasts and birds, tree-trunks and empty shells, and refreshed the countless subtleties of their fanciful imaginations with the realities of existence. It is true that they had a tendency to the monstrous and the distorted which offends our educated eye and better judgment : yet, some may still argue that their grotesque dragons and reptiles, their fish and gigantic birds, are but traditional representations of animals which, according not only to eastern story but to the facts made known by modern science, once trod and crawled upon the earth or swam across the seas.

Japanese porcelain bears a resemblance to that of China, but with a little experience can be easily distinguished. It is a more brilliant white and the clay is of a better quality; the designs are more simple and the decorations less overloaded; the animals are not so monstrous, and the flowers designed more in accordance with nature. Japanese porcelain does not stand the heat of the fire so well as the Chinese.

The oldest kind of Japanese ware is of a quaint shape with curious embossed figures, painted on a white ground in red and blue, the paste not being of a good quality. The most perfect production is the fine vitreous porcelain, the paste of which is prepared with extreme labour. It is so white and thin as to be perfectly translucent; the glaze so equal and clear and so colourless that one can scarcely believe it to be the work of the potter. The specimens brought to Europe have been mostly cups, with covers and saucers. The red Japan ware is a fine unglazed stone-ware like that afterwards imitated at Dresden by Böttcher.

Some very beautiful ware was also produced in Persia, and decorated with metallic lustres. It is made of very fine white paste, and the ornaments in perfect taste. Hunting scenes are a common subject, and especially flowers.

Vase, Persian porcelain.

It has long been an English taste to collect fine oriental china: and this was greatly influenced by Mary, queen of William the third. The correspondence and periodical literature of the last century are full of allusions to the mania for buying pieces of china; and the more hideous and outrageous the forms were, so much the more it was said they were sought after. This is a mere exaggeration: the fashion was a good fashion; and nothing could be more decorative than "the piles of china," "the chaos of Japan," "the pyramids of cups," "or the costly jars," which were so much complained of by writers in the Tatler or the Spectator. Of late years, in common with other things, prices have rapidly risen for really fine oriental porcelain. Egg-shell enamelled plates which twenty years ago might have been bought for £3 or £4 cannot now be purchased for five times the money; vases and sets of small pieces follow in the same proportion; and the very tall jars, for which £200 used to be thought to be an enormous sum, are worth £1000 and £1200 a pair. But it must be remembered that these great sums are to be obtained only for porcelain of the true date and highest quality. The market has been flooded with

POTTERY AND PORCELAIN.

inferior stuff, and unwary collectors have been terribly imposed upon.

The first porcelain works set up in England were at Chelsea and Bow. There seems to be no record of the precise dates of their establishment, nor of the names of the proprietors. They probably began about the year 1730, were in full work in 1745, and existed thirty or forty years.

Bow china was made at Stratford le Bow. It is often embossed and of quaint devices. The quality of the clay is inferior, and the paintings, on a plain ground, flowers or landscapes in bistre. A bee was occasionally placed in relief or painted on the handle or spout of a jug. The early specimens of Chelsea were painted to resemble oriental porcelain, and show a rudeness and want of finish usual in the first stage of any manufacture. The custom among German princes to attach china manufactories to their court no doubt influenced George the second to encourage the Chelsea works. He brought models and artists from Saxony, and enabled Chelsea to produce articles which rivalled in excellence and splendour the best importations from Dresden. Horace Walpole speaks of a service which he saw, intended as a royal present, which cost £1200. The Chelsea establishment was finally broken up about 1780, and the workmen and the models were transferred to Derby.

The first forms of Chelsea china are in a great degree after the French models. The colours are fine and vivid, bleu de roi, apple green, turquoise, and especially claret-colour, which seems to be peculiar to Chelsea. Many of the cabinet specimens approach the best productions of Sèvres in colour and painting. The porcelain from the softness of its paste will not bear any fresh exposure to the heat of a furnace, so that it cannot easily be repaired or (as they say) "doctored." The embossed oval with a raised anchor is generally considered as the earliest mark; afterwards the anchor was simply painted in red or gold; the gold anchor has no relation to the quality of the piece. Fine

Chelsea vase.

examples of Chelsea ware, especially vases, are very valuable and fetch high prices.

The Derby manufactory was founded in 1750, and in 1777 Dr. Johnson said that the china was beautiful, but so dear that he could have silver vessels made as cheap as those sold there of porcelain. Derby china is very transparent, and is characterised by a bright blue upon the border or edge of the tea-services; the ground is generally plain. The figures are not equal to those of Chelsea; but the white biscuit figures rival the biscuit of Sèvres. The secret of the Derby biscuit appears to have been lost: but the Parian has sprung from it. The marks are various; and lists are given in books upon the subject.

Plymouth china is very rare, and some of the best specimens

have great beauty and excellence of workmanship. The manufactory was established about 1760, and hard paste porcelain was there first made in England. The usual ornamentation consists of flowers, butterflies, birds, and monsters in rich colours, and sometimes with much gilding. A not uncommon characteristic is a crack in the glaze. The manufacture lasted only about twelve or fifteen years, and the proprietor's patent right was sold and transferred to Bristol. Bristol china consists mostly of tea and dessert services, figures, and bouquets of flowers, in the style of Vincennes. The common ware is generally blue and white, the best is rich in gilding and painting. The groups are inferior to Chelsea but better than those of Plymouth. The best known mark was a cross. Bristol china is also very rare; from the same cause as the Plymouth, the shortness of the time of production.

The Worcester works were begun about the year 1750; and the invention of printing upon the porcelain was almost contemporaneous. The china made from 1760 to 1770 was of very superior quality, and the colours used upon some of the ornamental pieces approached closely to the Chelsea, often in imitation of Japanese. The marks are of great variety, but denote the changes that have occurred in the ownership or direction and enable us to ascertain the dates of particular examples.

The first porcelain made at Worcester was what is called a frit body; that is, consisting of materials which are fritted or melted together at a great heat in order to form chemically that which we have naturally in the porcelain clays. The proportions of the Worcester body were the result of the scientific investigations of doctor Wall and no other artificial porcelain excels it, either in closeness of texture or perfect union with the glaze. It is said that no piece of old Worcester has been found *crazed*: a fault arising either, as in Chelsea sometimes, from excessive thickness of the glaze or, as in Derby, from a defect in the body.

The gilding of porcelain has always been one of the most important features in its decoration; and the preparation of the

Worcester gold was remarkable, rivalling some of the best continental work. Vienna and Sèvres surpass it; not so much perhaps on account of finer metal or better preparation, but from the more artistic and richer treatment. The principal colours of old Worcester are the fine cobalt blue, ruby, opaque green, and turquoise: and the cobalt blue has always been an especial favourite. The maroon specimens are scarce.

Without mentioning less noted places where porcelain has been made in England we must be content to add that manufactories were established in Wales; at Nantgaru or Nantgarrow in Glamorganshire and at Swansea. The wares once produced at these places were perhaps equal in quality to any china hitherto made in this country. No expense was spared in procuring workmen or materials; and the want of success must be attributed solely to the deficiency of public patronage. Since the discontinuance of these establishments the excellence of the ware has been more justly estimated, and prices are readily given by collectors much greater than those originally demanded.

Dish: Moustiers ware.

MAIOLICA.

Plate, 1520.

M. F. A.

MAIOLICA.

OTTERY and porcelain, in general, have been already spoken of at some length; but the Italian wares usually included under the name of Maiolica, that is, enamelled and painted earthenware, are so important that they deserve a further and separate notice. And first, with them, we must speak also of the productions of the Persian, Moorish, and Spanish potteries.

We are utterly ignorant at how early a date siliceous glazed tiles were used for wall decoration in the east. Bricks and fragments of tiles have been found among the ruins of some of the most ancient cities: and a piece of glazed pottery, supposed to have been of Hebrew manufacture, is preserved at Paris in the Louvre. Passing onwards, however, to a much later period we know that mosques in Persia, built in the twelfth century, are covered with enamelled tiles of beautiful workmanship and with lustred decoration.

If tiles of such excellence were made it is not to be doubted that potteries would also be established for the supply of vessels for domestic use and ornament; and, in fact, broken pieces of such ware and of like date have been found on the sites of nearly all the more important cities of Syria. When the Arabs invaded Europe and, known as Saracens, spread themselves along various parts of the shores of the Mediterranean and occupied Spain and the neighbouring islands, they brought with them their knowledge and skill in many oriental arts, and among these, of course, in pottery. Tile decorations were employed at a very early period in Spain, in the mosque at Cordova and other chief Moorish towns.

The principal divisions of the old eastern potteries are Persian, Damascus, and Rhodian wares. These were largely exported to

Rhodian shallow bowl.

the west of Europe, to France and England; and "Damas" cups and other vessels are mentioned in inventories of the fifteenth century. Very commonly, now, all examples of these different kinds in various collections are called Persian; it would be wiser to revive the old and better name of "Damascus ware." Early pieces are extremely scarce; the decoration is generally rich in colour, the ground white, blue or lilac, covered with panels of oriental form, or leafage, or large sprays of flowers, particularly

Persian wall tile.

roses, tulips, and carnations. The forms are elegant; large bowls on raised supports; bulb-shaped flasks with elongated necks; pear-shaped jugs, and circular dishes with deep centres.

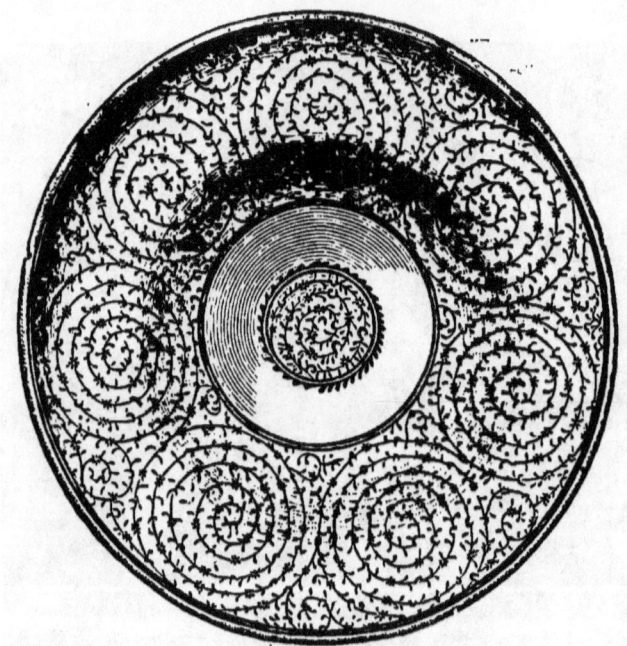

Early Damascus plate.

These have often Arabic or imitated Arabic inscriptions upon them; as in the vase engraved on the next page.

Until within the last twenty or thirty years the now clearly defined class of Hispano-moresque wares was indiscriminately grouped with the lustred maiolica of Italy; but more careful examination proved them to be of true Spanish origin. The correspondence of technical character with the " azulejos " (the well-known tiles which adorn the palace at Seville) and with the famous vase of the Alhambra, together with a marked difference between these and wares of ascertained Italian manufacture, led at last to the conviction that they must be the work of Moorish

MAIOLICA.

Vase, with imitated Arabic letters.

potters established in that country. Further enquiry led to the discovery also of important evidence on the point in contemporary documents. The only existing examples, however, of Saracenic pottery which can be assigned to any date earlier than the thirteenth century are the tiles, before mentioned, of the the mosque at Cordova.

The first, as it was the chief, site of the manufacture of Hispano-moorish ware was probably Malaga: and a native of

Tangier who travelled in Spain and wrote in the year 1350 states that "at Malaga the beautiful gilt pottery is made, which is exported to the most distant countries." We may not unreasonably suppose that the famous Alhambra vase was made there: at any rate this may be ascribed to about that date, from the style of its ornamentation and the character of the inscriptions. The vase was found with others, since destroyed, under the pavement of the Alhambra 300 years ago, and said to have been full of gold coins. A very important and splendid vase of the same period is in the Kensington museum: no. 8968, '63. Valencia was another town

Plateau, probably of Valencia.

where large quantities of "maiolica" were also made. The expulsion of the Moors from Spain, early in the seventeenth century, caused the extinction of all these works.

The potteries of Majorca and Sicily were also well known as early

Siculo-Moresque bowl.

as the fourteenth century: and it is generally agreed that the term *Maiolica* is derived, slightly altered, from the name of that island. In the same way, the word "china" is used in England to designate all kinds of porcelain, and "delft" for earthenware: China and Holland having been the countries from whence these varieties were originally imported. The early Italian potters learnt the process from Majorcan workmen, and then modified and improved it. The lustre colours of the Italian wares differ materially on the one hand from those of Spain, and on the other from that of Persia or of Damascus, taking an intermediate position and being superior in richness of effect.

There can be little doubt that from a very early period the Moorish pottery of the east, and from Spain and Sicily, was bought in Italy to a considerable extent. The brilliant prismatic hues by which it was distinguished must have excited general admiration. The existence of an active commercial intercourse between Spain and Italy in the middle ages is notorious, and the number of old pieces of Spanish origin still to be found in Italy is so great as alone to prove that there must have been, during the entire course of the fifteenth century, a constant competition between the Hispano-moresque wares and the advancing productions of Italian manufacture.

As long ago as the year 1350 it is said that potteries were also established at Pesaro, in the duchy of Urbino. The red clay, of which the wares were composed, was covered with a thin coating of very white earth, an "engobe" or "slip" which served as a ground for the patterns. The vessel was partly baked and then covered with lead glaze, after which it was again taken to the furnace for its final firing. This overlaying of an opaque white

Mezza-maiolica dish.

MAIOLICA.

substance may be considered as the starting point of maiolica. The colours employed were yellow, blue, and black: and the lead glaze imparted to the ware the iridescent lustre by which the mezza-maiolica, half or mixed maiolica (as it is called), was characterized.

It may still be a question by whom and in what country the stanniferous white enamel, which is an opaque glazing composed of tin, was discovered. In Italy the honour has always been given to Luca della Robbia, and although the use of this glaze may have been known before his time, it can scarcely be disputed that he not merely applied it to a new purpose, but that he really did invent an enamel of a peculiar whiteness and excellence, different in composition from any employed before. Moreover,

Medallion, by Luca della Robbia.

172   *MAIOLICA.*

we have no record or dated example of any Italian pottery coated with stanniferous enamel previous to the first known production in the year 1438.

Luca della Robbia was born about 1400 and lived until 1481; having first been bred up as a goldsmith, he applied himself to sculpture and then especially to modelling in relief in terra-cotta. After many experiments he found that if his figures in clay were coated over with a thick glaze of tin combined with other mineral substances, an almost endless durability might be secured to his works. His success was complete, and he may be said to have begun and completed his invention with one stroke. The

Virgin and Child; school of della Robbia; bas-relief.

MAIOLICA.

attitudes of his figures are always easy and the details quiet and simple; the framework of his compositions generally consisting of rows of small heads, angels or Cupids, or Greek friezes, or wreaths of flowers and fruits. For scenery, garments, and other accessories he used chiefly green, blue, and white; for more prominent effects gold, yellow, and violet. A remarkable peculiarity of his enamel is that, although from its transparency it betrays the red clay underneath, it assumes the appearance of yellow ivory. This is a good indication of the genuineness of any supposed work of the artist, and undisputed examples are excessively rare : probably very few exist out of Tuscany.

Luca della Robbia left a nephew, Andrea, who continued the works. He employed himself mostly in producing medallions, decorations for altars, and bas-reliefs generally. But his taste is less refined and his attitudes more stiff. By substituting fruits for flowers in the garlands which surround his pieces he gave them an appearance of heaviness. He was fond also of introducing the heads of cherubs in his design. After the death of Andrea his four sons succeeded, and in a short time the manufacture of the true della Robbia declined and became extinct.

Between 1450 and 1520 many pieces of maiolica were executed at Pesaro and Siena. The finest are those by an unknown artist about 1480. These dishes are usually of a flesh-coloured clay, thick, and of large size. The circular projection round the back is perforated very often with two holes, to admit a string for suspending them; being

Siena plate.

intended for show and not for use. The back is covered with a yellow glaze, and the front frequently with a portrait of some prince of the district. The colours are blue and yellow, and highly iridescent.

Dish; probably Pesaro.

After the death of Luca della Robbia the use of the white stanniferous enamel became general. Faenza was among the first places to adopt it, and the term "fayence" has been commonly used to describe earthenware. It is not certain, however, whether the term may not be more properly traced to a town in Provence, near Cannes, called Fayence; where potteries are stated to have existed from a very early period. We might here mention that other names have been also given as designations of maiolica. "Urbino" and "Umbrian" ware explain themselves as referring

Moulded dish; Faenza.

to those important sites of the manufacture : and " Raffaelle " ware doubtless from the many subjects after his designs and from the grotesques in his admirable style and manner.

Gubbio, a small town in the territory of the dukes of Urbino, is one of the most famous in the development of the art of pottery, as shown by works in maiolica. This excellence is to be attributed chiefly to the talent of one man, the maestro Giorgio Andreoli : and under his direction the furnaces at Gubbio produced examples of a special nature. The pieces were decorated with lustre pigments, flashing brilliant metallic ruby, golden, and opalescent tints which vary in every specimen and assume almost every colour of the rainbow, as they reflect the light directed at varying angles upon the surface.

Maestro Giorgio, born of a good family in Pavia, was an artist by profession, and seems to have settled at Gubbio about the year 1500. His first works were in the style of the della Robbia ;

Urbino dish, with Raffaellesque grotesques.

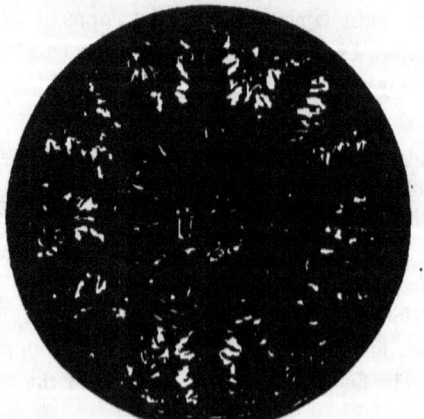

Lustred bowl; Gubbio.

and he is said to have made with his own hands two large altar pieces. It is very doubtful whether, as some insist, he invented

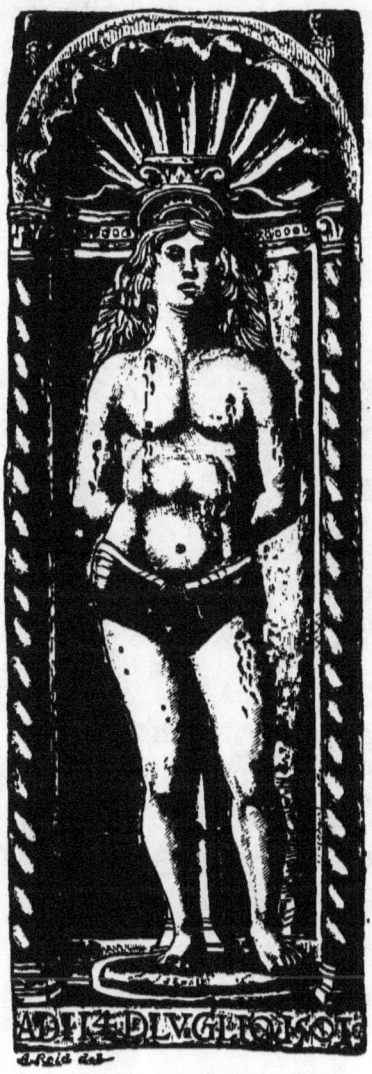

Early lustred plaque; by Giorgio?

the famous ruby lustre, or whether he brought the secret with him from Pavia: and, although his own work may be distinguished with approximate certainty, it is true that pieces signed by him were really painted by other hands. The best mark for recognition of a master's hand is faultless execution; and such we may say is the work of maestro Giorgio. The first dated piece which can be assigned to him is the relievo of St. Sebastian, at South' Kensington, no. 2601; marked with the year 1501: the earliest both signed and dated has two years named; 1517 and 1518. His signature varies much, as it occurs in successive years: his most beautiful productions were executed about 1525.

Deep dish; by Giorgio.

Maestro Giorgio's manner of decoration consists of foliated scrolls and other ornaments, terminating in dolphins, human heads, trophies, masks, etc; in the designing of which he exhibits very considerable power with great facility of invention. In the drawing of figures and of the nude he cannot be ranked as an artist of the first class. It is supposed that he was living in 1552.

Some of his assistants and his son Vincenzio continued the works after the death of Giorgio; but the excellence of the Gubbio maiolica gradually and rapidly diminished. About 1570 the employment of the lustres seems to have been almost discontinued; and the secret of their proper composition and manipulation was lost during the general decadence of Italian artistic pottery; at last the death of Guidobaldo II. in 1574 gave the finishing stroke to the already deteriorated wares of the duchy of Urbino.

Castel Durante produced excellent examples of maiolica.

Plate; Castel Durante.

These are generally to be recognized by a pale buff-coloured paste and great richness and purity of glaze. The plates are rarely decorated at the back but are usually edged with yellow on the subject-pieces, and with grey white on those having grotesques, which are in a low olive tint on a blue ground. Subject-pieces do not appear to have been so abundantly painted at Castel Durante as at other neighbouring places, and upon these an added lustre enrichment is even more rare. A very remarkable dish which may possibly be of this manufacture is at South Kensington; having in the centre a portrait of Perugino.

Dish, with portrait of Perugino.

The city of Urbino itself possessed at the same period works from whence issued some of the most famous and splendid examples of maiolica which are extant. Pottery of various kinds had been made there and in the neighbourhood from ancient times; but it was late in the fifteenth century before we can trace the manufacture of glazed or enamelled decorative wares. A very able artist and probably the first of eminence was Nicola da Urbino, from whose hand we have pieces as early as 1520. His manner is remarkable for a sharp and careful outline of the figures, with the features clearly defined and with much delicacy of touch; there is also a peculiar tightening of the ankle and rounding of the knee. His architecture is bright and distinct; the landscape back-ground carefully rendered in dark blue against a golden sky; the stems of the trees are strangely tortuous, coloured brown, and strongly masked with black lines. Possibly his best work was a service painted for Isabella d'Este, of which two plates are preserved in the British musuem. It is probable that few Maiolica painters have produced works of greater beauty

Dish; by Francesco Xanto.

than these, which are equally excellent in the quality of the glaze and brilliancy of colour.

Another well known artist of the Urbino potteries was Francesco Xanto, the dates of whose signed works extend from 1530 to 1542. His painted dishes and plates are to be seen in almost every large collection, and among them are examples of high excellence, although many betray a want of care and hasty execution. Some judges of much repute speak disparagingly of Xanto, as an artist monotonous and mechanical; and that his colouring is crude and full of violent opposition, the only merit being a certain force and brightness: but on the other hand some of his wares are profusely enriched with metallic lustres, including the ruby tint. It would be unfair to form a too severe opinion of the quality of Xanto's work, until after an examination of the brilliant dish at South Kensington, no. 1748, '55, painted with the marriage of Alexander and Roxana, after the picture by Raffaelle: see woodcut on preceding page.

But the celebrity of one family, the Fontana, and of one member of it in particular, Orazio, at Urbino, has been long established by common consent. These, father, sons, and grandchildren, manufactured maiolica for nearly a hundred years: from about 1510 to 1600. Specimens from the hands of one or other of the Fontana family are undoubtedly in many collections, but it is extremely difficult to appropriate them. The similarity of style and technical characteristics of several artists, working with the same colours on the same enamel ground, must necessarily resolve itself into a strong family resemblance. Some of the most celebrated pieces of the Fontana manufactory were made for the then duke of Urbino, and subsequently given to the Holy House at Loreto, where many of them are still preserved. It originally numbered 380 vases, etc., painted with subjects after designs by Raffaelle, Giulio Romano, and others. In more modern times a grand duke of Florence is said to have proposed to give in exchange for those at Loreto a like number of silver vessels of

Pilgrim's bottle; Fontana.

equal weight: and Louis the fourteenth to have offered copies of some of them in gold.

The process of making maiolica may be thus briefly described. The body of the ware, like that of all the mediæval pottery, is mere common clay or terra-cotta. When the piece is finished on the wheel and has taken its appointed shape, it is first thoroughly dried and then burnt in the furnace; in this state the ware is commonly termed "biscuit." The glaze is applied generally by immersion, that is, the substances composing it being reduced to a fine powder and mixed with water to the consistence of cream, the piece to be covered is dipped into this liquid. The porous nature of the biscuit speedily absorbs the moisture and the glazing adheres to the piece as a soft coating, liable to be removed by the lightest touch: on this surface the painting is executed with the enamel colours. It is here that the wonderful facility of the old Maiolica painters is displayed; the outlines must be drawn with a single stroke and not a touch can be erased. Even if the point of the brush be allowed to rest for a brief instant a blot instantly ensues. After the piece is painted it is again fired, enclosed now in a case of terra-cotta to protect it from the direct action of the flames. The crude glaze fuses into a glossy vitrified enamel and the painting, sinking into and becoming incorporated with it, assumes a degree of power and brilliancy of tint very different from its previous raw appearance.

There were several other places in Italy besides Pesaro, Gubbio, and Urbino where very admirable maiolica was made during the sixteenth century: at Forli, Caffaggiolo, Diruta, and Fabriano. Venice also must be especially mentioned. Though we have no sufficient record of their peculiar character we can have little doubt that wares were produced at Venice even earlier than the year 1500. On the other hand the best judges seem to agree that the glazed tiles in the sacristy of the church of Sta. Elena at Venice, which date about 1470, were importations from Faenza or Castel Durante. Whatever the truth may be the culminating period of the excellence of Venetian maiolica in respect to painting and design was the middle of the sixteenth century. Engraved is a very fine dish, of about the year 1540, now at South Kensington, no. 4438.

At Naples, in the seventeenth century some good maiolica was produced; and about the year 1740 the beautiful ware known as Capo di Monte. There is a truly original character

Dish, Venetian, at South Kensington.

about this porcelain. Shells and corals and embossed figures, exquisitely moulded in high relief, constitute its peculiar beauty and excellence. Capo di Monte china is exceedingly rare, very valuable, and to be found in few collections. Cups and saucers sold at the Bernal sale for £35 a pair; and a small snuffbox for £31. Modern imitations have been made in great quantities; but there is not much difficulty in distinguishing them from the genuine pieces.

It was commonly the habit of maiolica painters to affix marks or monograms; sometimes of individuals, sometimes of manufactories: family badges or trademarks seem also to have been transmitted from father to son. These signatures, however, do not appear to have followed any precise rule: often the signature of the master will be found on his least worthy productions whilst, by some caprice perhaps, his best works are left without any mark, and must be recognised only by the impress of the peculiar talent shewn in peculiarities of style which cannot be mistaken. Some artists seem to have consistently signed all their wares; for instance, it is rare to find any unsigned piece of Francesco Zanto; on the other hand, it is equally rare to meet with any signed example of the far greater Orazio Fontana. A very full list of the numerous marks upon maiolica is given by Mr. Fortnum, with fac-similes, in his detailed catalogue of the South Kensington collection.

Vase: at South Kensington, no. 500.

GLASS.

Cups, etc.; German.

(M. F. A.)

GLASS.

NO evidence or proof which may be relied upon reveals to us the time when the art of making glass was discovered, or the nation which first improved it. The old story told by Pliny is this: that some Phœnician merchants having disembarked near the mouth of the river Helus cooked their food upon the shore; and having piled up some lumps of natron (vitreous stone) upon the sand, the stones and the sand softening under the heat and mixing became a transparent and glassy mass. Chance probably did lead to the original production of this material, and there were various circumstances connected with very early manufactures, especially of pottery or the extraction of metals from their ores, which might have caused it. We must be content to learn that the art of glass making is to be traced to a most remote antiquity.

Egypt supplies us—as in many other branches of science and art—with the first positive evidences of glass-making. Sir Gardner Wilkinson speaks of glass bottles containing red wine represented on monuments of the fourth dynasty; more than four thousand years ago; and in the tombs of Beni-Hassan which date from the same period there are paintings which show the process itself of glass blowing. A glass bead has been found, bearing the name of a queen who reigned nearly fifteen hundred years before the Christian æra. Greek and Latin writers describe statues and obelisks ten, thirty, and even of sixty feet high made of one, three, or four emeralds: these were undoubtedly green glass.

Next in date to the earlier Egyptian examples is a vase of transparent greenish glass found at Nineveh, and now in the

British museum. On this is an inscription, bearing the name of a king who lived about B.C. 700. Fragments also of variously coloured glass have also been discovered there. Beads were, probably, among the first products of Egyptian or Phœnician workmen; and, as in modern times, were used for barter not only with the barbarous nations of the interior of Africa but with those of western Europe. One, of a Prussian blue colour, found in a very ancient British grave in Wiltshire, was analysed and ascertained to contain silica, potash, soda, alumina in small quantities, traces of lime and magnesia, oxide of iron and oxide of copper.

The Phœnicians and Egyptians carried their art into almost every country bordering upon the shores of the Mediterranean: and we can scarcely doubt that glass vessels were very anciently made in Greece, in the islands of the Archipelago, in Etruria, and in Sicily. The beautiful little vases which may be seen in almost every national collection, and which have been found in the cemeteries of Italy and Greece, have however a similarity of character which would lead us to suppose that they were brought from a few chief centres of the manufacture. These vases are of different colours, generally blue; usually with surfaces ornamented by bands of white, yellow, or turquoise forming zigzag lines, incorporated with the surface though not penetrating through the entire thickness. The form of by far the greater number is Greek rather than Egyptian or any other oriental type.

It has been said by some authors that glass was not imported into Rome until the time of Sylla; be this as it may, it is certain that the art of glass making had made great progress before the reign of Augustus, and vessels of all kinds, whether for use or decoration, were in high estimation. Glass has been found in windows at Pompeii. The Romans knew how to stain glass, to blow it, to work it on a lathe, and to engrave it. Perfect examples of fine Roman glass are, as may easily be understood from its fragile nature, of extreme rarity: but the quantity once existing there in the first and second centuries must have been enormous; prodigious numbers of fragments—and these of pieces rivalling in excellence of workmanship the most famous which have been preserved—are dug up year after year in the city or in the neighbourhood of Rome.

A large proportion of antique Roman glass is found to be brightly iridescent, displaying all the colours of the rainbow with dazzling intensity; red, orange, green, and pink shining out in prismatic colours, like the inside of a pearl oyster shell. This iridescence is caused by a decomposition of the outer surface.

We have more than one record in the old historians of the large sums paid by wealthy men in imperial times for glass cups and vases; such, for example, as the 6000 sertertia which Nero gave for two small vases : and the good taste of a people so highly civilised and so luxurious naturally led them to value cups of glass, the work of artists, far beyond those which were made simply of mere gold or silver. That this admiration and judgment were well founded is clear to us even now from one or two celebrated examples still remaining; such as the Portland vase in the British museum or the vase in the Museo Borbonico at Naples.

We learn from Pliny that many varieties of coloured glass were made by the Romans in his time; he speaks of opaque red, of white, of black (like obsidian), of glass imitating jacinths, sapphires and other gems, and of murrhine glass. These varieties occur in every large collection of antique glass, except (so far as we know) the murrhine; about which and its true character there has long been much dispute. Some have thought it to have been an imitation of fluor spar, some that it was not glass at all but a kind of agate, or fluor spar itself.

The Roman artist worked not only with glass of various colours but of many shades of the chief colours, blending them in the same piece in almost every conceivable combination; sometimes so as to traverse and be mixed together in the entire substance of the object, sometimes by the placing of the one colour over the other. In the first class we must put those pieces which we call mosaic or *mille fiori* (where the process of manufacture was by uniting the threads of glass by heat into a rod, which when cut transversely showed the same pattern in every section); or vases with wavy bands of colour, or imitating porphyry or serpentine, or vessels with interlacing threads. Gold leaf also was sometimes introduced. In the second class are the cameo glasses, like the Portland vase, in which a paste of one colour is superimposed upon another and then carved into the required design. Perfect examples are very rare; and all, even the fragments of the same kind, are remarkable for their beauty; the ground is generally blue, often transparent, sometimes opaque; and the upper layer which is sculptured is usually opaque white. In the same class we must place, but at a long interval, the glass vessels which are ornamented with coarse threads trailed over their surfaces to form rude patterns or with coloured enamels.

In the third and following centuries pictorial representations were made by means of gold leaf, either embedded in the substance of the glass or fixed to the surface. Many of them have been found in the catacombs, in consequence of the Christian practice of attaching the disks, which formed the bottoms of vessels thus ornamented, to the compartments in which the dead were placed. It is very seldom that the vessels themselves are found entire; the few which exist are shallow bowls.

Rare as perfect examples are which have been preserved of antique Roman glass, still more rare are any pieces which we can certainly attribute to workmen of the eastern empire. We know that at Constantinople glass-making was carried on to a great extent; one of the gates took its name from the adjacent quarter where the glass houses were; but we can point to scarcely a single specimen of undoubted Byzantine art from the fourth to the fourteenth century. Two bowls in the British museum may be Byzantine, on one of which is a Greek inscription: and at Venice in the treasury of St. Mark's are some cups and basins, decorated in a style very similar to other objects of Byzantine art, and traditionally said to have been brought from Constantinople by the crusaders about the year 1200. The Holy Dish preserved at Genoa and long believed to be an emerald, is possibly Byzantine glass; the colour is fine but contains many small bubbles; the shape hexagonal, with some slight ornament. This famous dish was part of the plunder brought from Cæsarea in 1101.

Nor do we know where to look for existing examples of glass which we can attribute with any degree of certainty to European manufacture during the same centuries.

The knowledge of the process of making both plain and coloured glass was however diffused throughout Europe from a period at least as early as the twelfth century. This is proved by the treatises of Eraclius and Theophilus, who describe various methods both of making and of ornamenting glass; nor is it probable that the art at any time was altogether lost in any country of the west. Of purely oriental work there is a Persian specimen, of the sixth century, in the public library at Paris; a shallow gold bowl, partly ornamented with rosettes and lozenges of green and white glass. To a later time we can attribute a few known specimens; and more particularly the large enamelled glass lamps which were suspended in mosques, some of which have dates reaching back to the end of the thirteenth century. These show that the makers were expert glass blowers and could produce works of considerable size. Cups and other vessels of this manufacture were brought to western Europe, and are mentioned in mediæval inventories as "of the fashion of Damascus," or as painted "à la Morisque;" and a few examples have been preserved to our own days. Among them, the cup in the museum at Breslau, said to have belonged to St. Elizabeth of Hungary who died in 1281; a cup (so called) "of Charlemagne," at Chartres; and possibly the well-known "Luck of Eden Hall" still kept by the Musgrave family, are oriental glass.

Enamelled Oriental glass.

Two of the most authentic and most precious specimens of eastern glass which now exist uninjured were shown at Vienna in the exhibition there in 1860. These, so long ago as 1373, were particularly mentioned in an inventory of the treasures of the church of St. Stephen as "two bottles from Damascus." One of them has two handles, and is decorated with interlaced zones alternately with a ground work of little rosettes of gold, edged with coloured enamel. The other has a frieze of little draped figures, four separate medallions, and the mysterious emblem, the sacred tree.

Even when we pass on through the next two or three centuries we are scarcely able to refer to a single specimen of vessels of glass,

GLASS.

which has come down to our time. One or two pieces may perhaps exist in conventual and church treasuries which have been parts of reliquaries, and old records occasionally mention them. But the use of painted glass for windows began about the eleventh, and reached its utmost perfection during the next three or four centuries. Great authorities agree that the earliest date to be given to pictorial representations, properly so called, on window glass is later than the year 1000; and it is believed that no more ancient monument of the art is known. All windows before that time, if coloured in any way, were ornamented merely by small pieces arranged, as a mosaic, in simple geometrical patterns.

It must be remembered that there is a great difference between colouring glass and painting upon it. The coloured glass is obtained by a mixture of metallic oxides whilst in a style of

Stained glass; fifteenth century.

fusion. This colouring pervades the substance of the glass and becomes incorporated with it. To paint glass the artist uses a plate of translucent glass, either colourless or already tinted, and applies the design and colouring with vitrifiable colours on one or both surfaces. These colours, true enamels, are the product of metallic oxides combined with vitreous compounds called fluxes. The fluxes serve as vehicles and through their medium, assisted by a strong heat, the colouring matters are fixed upon the plate.

Throughout the mediæval ages the tints of each part of the design were composed of pieces of stained glass of the required colours, cut to shape and joined with narrow strips of lead, the main lines of the design being necessarily formed by the lead, whilst the shading and other details were painted in bold lines, hatchings, or stipplings of opaque dark brown. England, France, and Flanders supply us with the most admirable examples

Flemish; about 1520.

of mediæval painted windows, in perfect harmony with the general effect of the buildings to which they belong: in Italy they are comparatively rare, and probably none before the middle of the thirteenth century. In 1295 English records speak of glass painters as among chief tradesmen; particularly at Colchester, where the sand is of a suitable kind, and the salt marshes would furnish abundance of plants whose ashes yield the necessary alkalies.

In France probably no painted windows of the thirteenth century exceed those which are in the Sainte Chapelle at Paris. These windows are large, and are filled with dark and rich glass in order to subdue the light. They contain, it is said, about eight hundred subjects and two or three thousand figures. The drawing is good; the faces expressive; and the draperies well arranged.

The elaborate medallion windows were generally reserved for large churches and cathedrals; in smaller buildings their place was supplied by the *grisaille* windows. In the fourteenth century the window divided into a number of small compartments superseded the old medallion arrangement, and the subjects were piled one upon another with occasionally a flat canopy. At the period of the renaissance the best masters were employed to make cartoons; enamel was used to give depth to the colours without losing richness, and more white was employed. Some very fine examples, from Flemish designs, are known in England of about that date: among others, at Fairford in Gloucestershire, and at University college, in Oxford. Towards the beginning of the seventeenth century the art declined.

The chief seat of the manufacture of vessels of glass and personal ornaments of the greatest beauty and excellence for many generations was Venice, and "Venetian glass" has long held a world-wide renown. Much obscurity remains as to when the glass works were first established there; but there can be little doubt that the taking of Constantinople in 1204 gave the Venetians the opportunity of acquiring additional knowledge of the art. At any rate we find that in 1268 the manufacture was so important

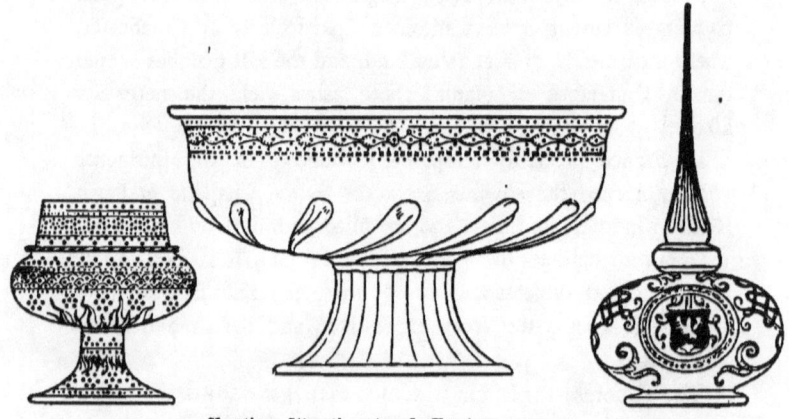

Venetian; fifteenth century? Kensington museum.

that the glass makers were already collected into a corporation. After that time we can produce an uninterrupted series of acts of the Venetian government, proving the great importance of the glass works and the interest taken in them by the state. So rapidly did the manufactories multiply that the city, before the century ended, was dangerously exposed to frequent fires, and decrees were passed ordering them to be removed out of it. Choice was then made of the island of Murano, separated from Venice by a small canal; and in a few years the whole island was covered with glass houses of various descriptions.

During the fourteenth century beads, false stones, and imitations of jewels, rather than cups and the like, seem to have been the chief productions of the Venice workman. No vessels have yet been described which can be attributed to an earlier time; most probably these were also made, but have perished. Bottles and cups ornamented by spiral lines may be seen in some very

GLASS.

old Italian pictures. Among the best and earliest known examples of Murano workmanship are a cup of blue glass (in the museum at Venice) enamelled and gilt with portraits in medallions, and ascribed to about the year 1440; and two admirable pieces in the British museum, standing cups, the one of a rich emerald green, the other of a fine sapphire hue: both, partly gilded and with subjects painted in enamel. These are part of the Slade collection, and were bought at prince Soltykoff's sale a few years ago, the first for nearly £250 and the other for £200. Gilding and decorations in enamel colours are very frequent on Venetian glass of this period, and scalework or an imbricated pattern in gold with points of enamel colours in imitation of jewels is a characteristic style. Probably this taste was prompted by the oriental enamelled

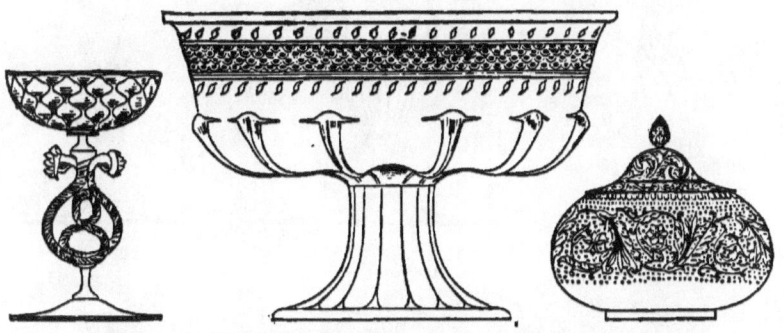

Venetian; old enamelled: Kensington museum.

glass wares which, as already observed, were perhaps generally known in Europe during the middle ages.

Venetian glass is usually of extreme thinness, being nearly always blown; and there is an endless variety to be found in the shapes and in the application of colour. Glass blowing, like throwing clay on the potter's wheel, induces beautiful curved forms and tenuity of substance, and as a rule Venetian glass is

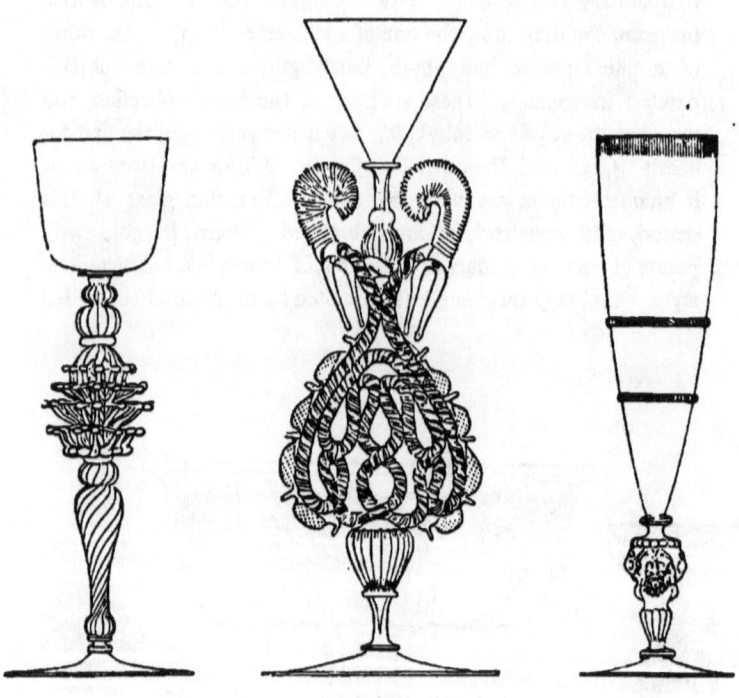

Venetian glasses.

consistently characterized by adherence to the natural suggestions of the material. This character and these forms—almost boundless in variety owing to the fertility of Venetian imagination —are far more suitable to the nature of glass than the more modern taste which imitates crystal. Glass is formed by the combination of silicic acid with certain metallic oxides, producing compounds which fuse into colourless transparent liquids, and

GLASS.

finally cool into hard, brittle, solids of a non-crystalline character. Any attempt to give glass the appearance of cut crystal is to treat it, so far, in a manner foreign to its real nature. (The following woodcuts show examples of old glass in the Kensington museum, of different kinds; the forms, not the colours: nor, strictly, according to the divisions to which they are attached.)

Mr. Franks has well arranged Venetian glass in six divisions; namely,

1st. Vessels of colourless or transparent glass, or of single colours; that is, glass coloured with metallic oxides before being worked. Clear white glass is commonly used for drinking cups,

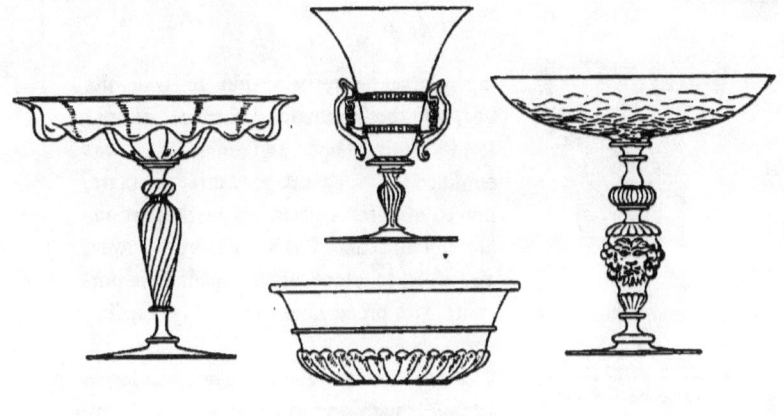

Cups, etc.

but they are not unfrequently decorated with coloured glass laid on externally, or forming part of the ornaments of the stems. The coloured glasses are generally blue or purple.

2nd. Gilt and enamelled glass. These methods of decoration were employed in the fifteenth century on both coloured and uncoloured glass, and the cups or vases are rather massive. A little later when extreme lightness and elegance of form were sought after, the drink-

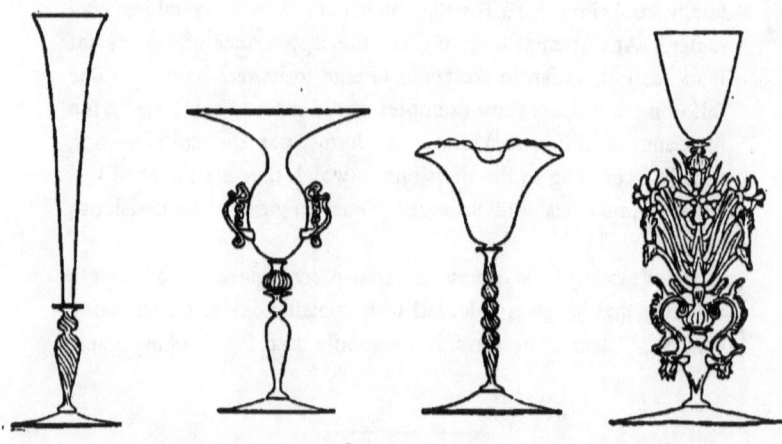

Cups, etc.

Cup; green enamelled.

ing glasses were too thin to bear the heat of the enamelling furnace without losing their shape, and enamelling was confined in a great measure to tazze, bowls, and salt-cellars. The decorations are chiefly coats of arms or merely flowers and dots, in place of the medallion portraits or processions of the preceding age.

3rd. Crackled glass. This, having a surface rough and divided irregularly by ridges, is supposed to have been made by suddenly cooling the vessel when half blown, and then reheating and expanding it, so as to increase the distance between the sections into which the surface was cracked by the sudden change of temperature. It is believed to date from the sixteenth century.

4th. Variegated or marbled opaque glass, generally known as *schmelz*. The most common variety is a mixture of green and purple, sometimes resembling jasper, sometimes chalcedony.

Other varieties are imitations of lapis lazuli and tortoise shell. Avanturine, which is obtained by mingling metallic filings or small fragments of leaf-gold with melted glass, may be included in this division, and patches of it are found mixed with schmelz.

5th. Millefiori or mosaic glass. This is made from sections of the canes or rods, which exhibit patterns; and are imitations of the old Roman process, but not executed with the same taste and success.

Clear, with ornaments and blue bands.

Cups, etc.

6th. Reticulated, filigree, or lace glass. The varieties contain fine threads of glass, generally coloured but sometimes milk-white, included in their substance; and are among the most beautiful of the products of the skill of Murano. The outline of the process

Cup; reticulated.

is this:—canes were prepared enclosing threads of opaque white or coloured glass; these were placed side by side in a mould, and a thin bubble of glass blown into the midst so as to adhere to the canes; the whole was once more heated and formed into a hollow cylinder, which was then fashioned in the same manner as any ordinary glass. A still further intricacy was obtained by using two cases or cylinders, the lines of which ran in contrary directions; when one of these was placed inside the other and the two welded together a reticulated pattern was produced.

It is well known that the lightness and strength of the Venetian glass are due to its not containing lead like our modern flint glass; and this lightness enabled the makers to give us the marvels of delicacy and beauty which we admire so much. Constant care was taken to keep the processes of the manufacture secret, and we are at this day ignorant of many of the details which belonged

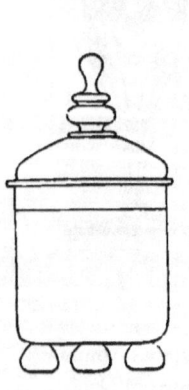 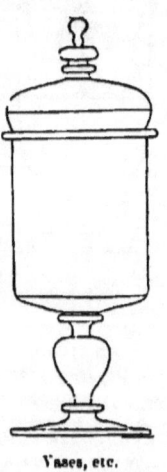 

Vases, etc.

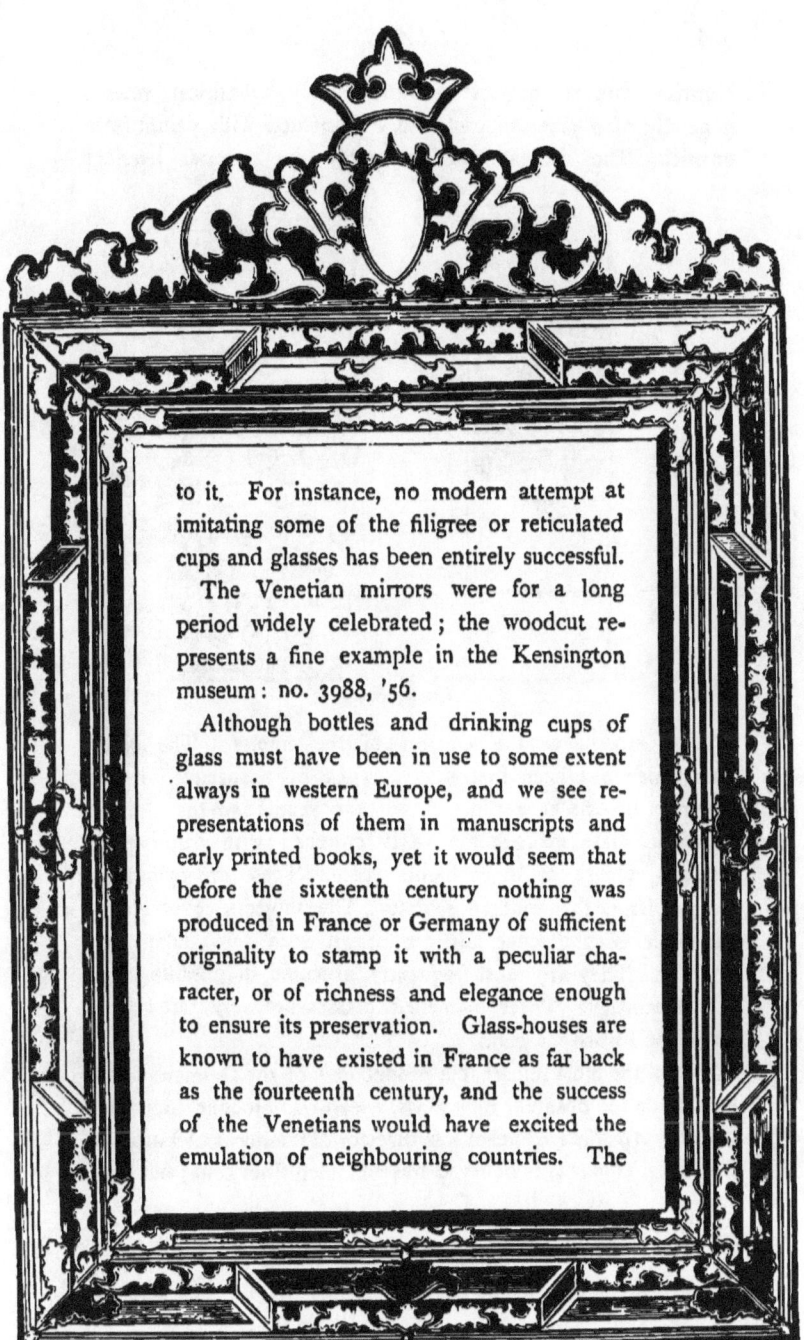

to it. For instance, no modern attempt at imitating some of the filigree or reticulated cups and glasses has been entirely successful.

The Venetian mirrors were for a long period widely celebrated; the woodcut represents a fine example in the Kensington museum: no. 3988, '56.

Although bottles and drinking cups of glass must have been in use to some extent always in western Europe, and we see representations of them in manuscripts and early printed books, yet it would seem that before the sixteenth century nothing was produced in France or Germany of sufficient originality to stamp it with a peculiar character, or of richness and elegance enough to ensure its preservation. Glass-houses are known to have existed in France as far back as the fourteenth century, and the success of the Venetians would have excited the emulation of neighbouring countries. The

Mirror frame.

German work is the best known; chiefly cylindrical vessels, generally of a greenish cast and ornamented with paintings in enamel. The designs are commonly the armorial bearings

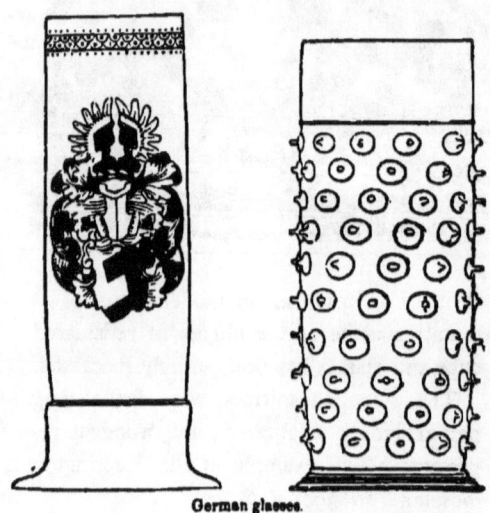

German glasses.

of the emperor or the electors of the empire. The oldest date which has been met with is 1553 on a specimen in the Chamber of Arts at Berlin. About the year 1650 the German artists in glass made some vases enriched with paintings in vitreous colours, of a far higher value. These are cylindrical and not larger than modern goblets. The subjects cover almost the whole circumference, and are drawn with much talent and delicacy. They are most frequently executed in grisaille or in brown camaïeu. These enamelled glasses are very rare; three are in the British museum.

One of the most remarkable productions of the German manufactories is the beautiful ruby glass, which was brought to perfection in 1679 when Kunckel was director of the works at Potsdam. The finest colour it is believed was obtained from gold; but it is

Vases, etc.; German.

now known that it can be got also from copper though the manipulation is difficult, a little more or less heat giving very different tints. From the beginning of the seventeenth century the Bohemian manufactories supplied vases of good form, which were enriched with ornamental subjects, particularly with portraits engraved upon the glass.

The art of wheel engraving upon glass was much employed in France. The goblets especially, generally of a simple form, which are ornamented with monograms and initial letters interlaced in the midst of an escutcheon are well known. The most

German, with raised bosses, dated 1643.   Ruby glass; Bohemian.   Bohemian clear glass.

delicate of these are of the time of Louis the sixteenth. In our own days the discovery of an exceedingly powerful chemical agent has made this kind of ornamentation very popular and less costly. This agent is hydrofluoric acid which eats into the surface of the glass, following the prescribed pattern already traced upon it, and scoops out the lines of the design.

The earliest positive evidence which we have of glass making in England seems to be in 1447, when John Prudde of Westminster engaged to execute the windows of the Beauchamp chapel at Warwick, and to use " no glasse of England." Fuller, writing in 1662, asserts that " coarse glass making was in Sussex of great antiquity." Many years before this, Stow tells us that ",the first making of Venice glasses in England began in London, about the beginning of the reign of queen Elizabeth, by one Jacob Vessaline, an Italian;" and the manufacture during that reign must have reached a certain amount of importance, because "glasses of English making" are included in the list of articles proposed by Richard Hakluyt to be carried with the expedition for finding Cathay in 1580. The site of a glass manufactory, apparently of that date and of which some of the productions seem to have been in the style of Murano, was discovered in 1860 at Buckholt farm, about nine miles from Salisbury. In 1670 the duke of Buckingham brought workmen from Venice and established them at Lambeth: from whence came many of the mirrors with bevelled edges, still remaining in old-fashioned houses.

We slightly referred above to the Portland vase in the British museum: this is a piece so famous, and so worthy of careful examination by every student, that we shall give a brief description of it. It was found in a sarcophagus at Rome; and is a vessel with two handles about ten inches high, of transparent dark blue glass coated with a layer of opaque white glass which has been treated as a cameo; the white glass having been cut down, so as to give on each side groups of figures admirably executed in relief. The subject is the marriage of Peleus and Thetis. A vase of smaller size but of similar style is in the museum at Naples; this was found at Pompeii.

The Chinese and Japanese must have been for a long time acquainted with the art of making glass in order to obtain the vitreous colours employed in their enamels and porcelain. We do not know, however, any examples which can certainly be referred to any great antiquity: and there is no doubt that the greater portion of glass to be found in China comes from abroad. The distinguishing feature of Chinese glass is want of clearness. A thin and tough variety found in the northern districts resembles Venetian glass; and the similarity may be due to early importations by travellers from the west.

Before we conclude our remarks we would quote an interesting note from a manuscript journal of the 17th century. An Englishman, a "travelling tutor" (as he calls himself) speaks of the famous glass houses which he saw at Venice in 1650; after describing the mirrors he tells us "the Italians have glasses that are almost as large and flat as silver plates, and almost as uneasy to drink out of."

Window glass; English, about 1500.

MOSAICS.

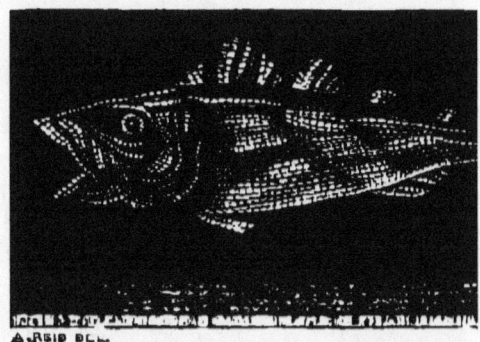

Ancient Roman; Kensington museum.

M. F.

MOSAICS.

Y mosaic, in the widest sense of the word, is to be understood the art of producing a design or painting by the joining together of small pieces of hard substances, either naturally or artificially coloured. Hard stones, marbles, and glass are the materials most frequently used in this kind of work. We may make, further, two subdivisions, differing according to the nature of the process. One, mosaics properly so called; the combination of many pieces by which a decorative surface is constructed. The other, inlays, in which various figures or spaces are cut out of a ground, and filled in with another substance or with different tints of the same material. There are almost endless varieties of both kinds.

This art of putting together small cubes or *tesseræ*, as they are technically called, either in monochrome or in different colours, is of very ancient date; and was known to the Egyptians and the Assyrians. We have positive evidence from the character of painted Egyptian ornaments and the actual existence of many of their peculiar little amulets, that mosaic, in its minor form at least, was made perhaps in the time of the Pharaohs and certainly before the Ptolemaic æra. Some Assyrian fragments brought from Nimroud include a few beautiful specimens, now in the British museum, inlaid in ivory, exactly of a mosaic pattern. The tesseræ are minute, somewhat resembling the modern Roman mosaic; the colours green, white, and red divided by gold lines. It is clear that flooring of this sort was known in the days of Ahasuerus from a verse in the book of Esther, which tells us of beds of gold and silver in the palace of Shushan "upon a pavement red and blue and white marble."

In Greece mosaic pavements were laid down in the age of Alexander, and modern writers have referred to passages in ancient authors which would show that the ornamentation bestowed on the ground even excelled that spent upon the walls and ceilings. A curious anecdote has been quoted from one of them who relates that Diogenes, the cynic, having gone into a private house, adorned with a magnificent pavement on which were figured all the Olympian deities, turned round and spat in the owner's face; excusing himself by saying (in the way of further compliment) that it was the least noble spot he could find in the whole house.

The first authentic account to be found of any mosaic work in ancient Rome is given us by Pliny; who says that Sylla caused some "stone-laid" work to be made: and from his and other sources of evidence we are justified in assuming the time of its introduction to have been about eighty years before Christ. This date corresponds with the destruction of Corinth, when precious objects of all kinds were carried to Rome: and naturally created a wish in the minds of wealthy Romans to possess mosaics as well as other luxurious embellishments.

A very learned Italian writer has divided Roman mosaics into four classes: namely, tesselated and sectile, applied to pavements generally; fictile and verniculated or pictorial, applied to walls and vaults. Of these, the tesselated is probably the most ancient and consisted of small cubes of marble, seldom averaging more than three-quarters of an inch square, worked by hand into such simple geometrical figures as, when combined, would best compose a larger figure, equally geometrical but of course more intricate. It is probable that the first colours used were chiefly black and white. The best examples of this tesselated work occur at Pompeii and at the baths of Caracalla; but very fine specimens have been found in this country. The sectile or sliced work was formed, some say, of the different slices of marble of which figures and ornaments were made; others hold that these slices were never employed to imitate figures or any actual subject, but produced their effect solely through the shape, colour, and vein of the marbles which were contrasted. It is believed that no piece or fragment of ancient sectile work imitating a subject of any kind has yet been found; and if it had been so employed we must have had examples at Pompeii, where the student may find all varieties of mosaic pavement known to either Greek or Roman. The most noble specimen of sectile work now extant is the splendid pavement of the Pantheon at Rome, where the principal marbles are arranged, each of great superficial extent, in alternate round and square slabs. The building of the Pantheon was finished about thirty years before the Christian æra. This kind of work required the employment of costly marbles, and no remains of it have been discovered in any other country than in Italy.

The fictile work was composed of small portions of mixed silex and alumina, coloured by the addition of one of the metallic oxides. The principal advantages offered by this material were that it could be obtained of any variety of colour, from the most delicate to the most intense; that it could be easily reduced to any given form; that it was far less costly than the precious marbles; and, lastly, that it could be covered with an untarnishable gilding. Hence, it speedily arrived at universal popularity; and the "vitreæ parietes," or glassy walls, were the prevailing decorations of Roman houses from the earliest imperial times. The following was the process adopted for the production of the gold grounded tesseræ, existing at Pompeii. On a piece of vitreous compound—in shape and size a thin tile and unburnt—a sheet of glass was laid, and over that a piece of gold leaf covered by another sheet of very fine glass; the whole being then placed in a kiln was burnt to such a point as to render the union of the parts perfect, and make the whole tile homogeneous in substance. It was then broken up into the required sizes.

The "*opus vermiculatum*" or vermiculated work, the most elaborate of the four varieties, was applied to the direct imitation of figures, ornaments, and pictures; the entire subject being portrayed in its true shades and colours, by a judicious arrangement of small cubes of different coloured marbles; and where extreme brilliancy was required by the aid of gems, and pieces of fictile work. This kind of mosaic may be divided into three subdivisions, not of difference of work but of scale. The larger or "opus majus" was generally employed for large pavements or ceilings, and represented figures of gods and centaurs or the like, commonly in white and black marble only. Very admirable specimens have been found, especially in the baths of Caracalla, executed with wonderful spirit; the cubes, however, are very large, and the work coarse. In the "*opus majus*" though the stones used are not always of a regular shape they more nearly approach the square than in any of the smaller styles. The ancient examples of this work, being always drawn well and boldly, produce at a proper distance from the eye an excellent effect.

The *medium* or middle style of mosaic was a much finer kind of work, and such subjects were generally executed in it as demanded greater delicacy in the treatment and softness in the shades and tints; cupids and children for example, flowers, and festoons. It is probable that "medium" mosaic was adopted chiefly in decorating walls; but some beautiful specimens have been found at Pompeii, where they were used as pavements in the chief parts of the house. The great Pompeian mosaic now in the Vatican, "the battle of Issus," is of this work: and a finely executed head of Minerva, also in the Vatican.

But the "*minus opus vermiculatum*" was the most delicate and elaborate of all the ancient Roman mosaics, and consisted of pictures formed of minute pieces of marble and fictile work; many of the little strips being less than the twentieth of an inch across. We might easily suppose that mosaics of so delicate a

From the "Battle of Issus."

workmanship would always have been regarded—as we now regard pictures—as portable furniture; but several examples of great beauty have been discovered at Pompeii inserted in the pavements. The best known from frequent copies, and by far the most exquisite specimen of this art now existing, is the mosaic usually called "Pliny's doves." The original alone can give us an accurate notion of the taste and beauty which it displays. It is preserved in the museum of the Capitol and represents a metal basin, on the edge of which four doves are sitting; one of them stooping to drink. The execution of the plumage is most minute and as refined as the whole idea and composition are captivating and graceful. This exquisite relic was found in the gardens of Hadrian's villa at Tivoli, in 1737.

The cement commonly used by the ancients consisted of a mixture of slaked lime and powdered marble, blended with water and the whites of eggs. This "marmoratum" (as it was called) was intensely hard and set almost immediately; so that it was impossible to make alterations in the work without destroying great portions. To compose the bed a layer of large stones or flints, with very little cement, was first placed upon the ground. Upon this was spread a coarse concrete, of smaller stones and lime, which was beaten and pressed down with much care until its thickness was reduced from one foot to nine inches. The third layer was a cement composed of one part lime and three of broken brick, shards, etc., worked to a true face upon which was drawn the outline of the design. The tesseræ or small pieces

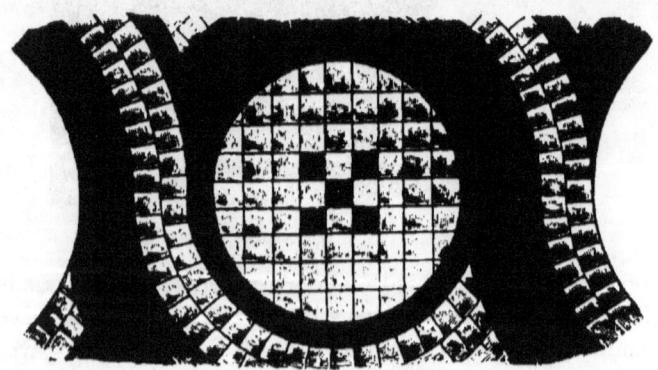

Antique Roman mosaic: Kensington museum.

were then arranged in their proper places, and over all was poured liquid cement to fill up the interstices. Afterwards all inequalities were reduced by friction, and the whole brought to one uniform surface.

From the examples still existing the art would appear to have reached its highest perfection during the second century, and almost every important building employed this embellishment. Scarcely a house of any size at Pompeii was without some kind of tesselated pavement; and wherever Roman colonization extended we find traces of mosaic. Not to speak of other countries, many examples have been discovered in England. A few are preserved in the British museum: the best is a small portion of the great Woodchester pavement. Early in the third

From Woodchester.

century the art seems to have lost in quality what it gained in quantity.

In examining ancient mosaics, whether pictorial or imitative, the student will be amazed with the wide range embraced and the evidence of intellect displayed in the selection of the various subjects. Gods, centaurs, men, animals, landscapes, flowers, foliage, are depicted with equal ability; and we must remem-

Antique mosaic panel: Kensington museum.

ber that we are indebted to the durability of the materials for the preservation of many of the lovely fancies of the great artists of antiquity. When we regard, moreover, the appropriation of these subjects and their relation to the positions for which they were intended, we are struck with the general congruity existing between the design and the character of the apartment to be adorned. Thus, in the houses at Pompeii we find the dog guarding the threshold or the hospitable invitation "salve" in the doorway: in the hall is a rich though simple pattern: in the dining-room representations of fragments of food: in the women's apartments composition of ornaments, animals, and foliage of the greatest delicacy. As Sir Digby Wyatt well says, "What a lesson should this afford to those who daily heap together in the decoration of their apartments the most incongruous ideas and the least harmonious associations,—who place an Annunciation in a dining-room, flanked by a sporting print and the portrait of a gentleman!"

From mosaic at Avignon.

From the middle of the fourth century when Christianity began rapidly to spread over Europe, and the seat of empire had been removed to Constantinople, the oriental taste for gold and splendour superseded the purer practice of the Romans, and Byzantine glass mosaic started into life. There is every reason to believe that the Greeks for many centuries were almost the exclusive workers in mosaic, and through their ingenuity Italy and Sicily stand pre-eminent in the possession of churches and baptisteries, adorned with the gilded ground and the gorgeously draped and swarthy visaged saints peculiarly Byzantine. The pieces of glass used in this work are of very irregular shapes and sizes, of all colours and tones of colour, and the ground tint almost invariably prevailing is gold. The manner of execution is always large and coarse, rarely approaching in neatness of joint and regularity of bedding even the old "opus majus vermiculatum." Yet, says Sir Digby Wyatt, the effect of splendid, luxurious, and at the same time solemn decoration is unattainable by any other means which he has found employed in structural embellishment.

The most ancient glass mosaics, which either exist or of whose existence we have sufficient evidence, possess an extraordinary interest: they have supplied probably the first type for the appearance of our Saviour. One is said to have been executed as early as the first century: and another, of the fourth century, was found in the cemetery of San Calisto at Rome, and is now preserved in the Vatican. The pious duty of imitating these mosaic pictures afterwards was one of the chief causes of the general resemblance of physiognomy and the peculiar Byzantine character of the head, in many of the portraits of our Lord dating from that period to the tenth century. Reproductions of the Ravenna and some other renowned mosaics of the early period are in the South Kensington museum.

Another variety of Christian mosaic consisted in the insertion into grooves cut to the depth of about half an inch in white marble of small cubes of coloured and gilded "smalto;" (as the Italians call the material of which mosaic is composed;) and in the arrangements of them in such geometrical combination as to make most elaborate patterns. This decoration was chiefly employed for church purposes: for screens, pulpits, episcopal thrones, and ciboria or tabernacles. Such work was very rarely used externally.

The earliest specimen is believed to be the chair and tribune in the church of San Lorenzo at Rome, made probably about the year 580.

Towards the beginning of the thirteenth century the Italians began to learn how to execute mosaic work for themselves. The names of several great artists are on record: the last, perhaps, was the celebrated Gaddo Gaddi, who was summoned to Rome

MOSAICS. 223

where he made, among other large undertakings, the great mosaic still existing on the façade of the church of Santa Maria Maggiore. With him the genuine art of Italian glass mosaic may be said to have ended, although small portions of later date are to be found at St. Mark's at Venice.

Scarcely any examples of this art are to be found out of

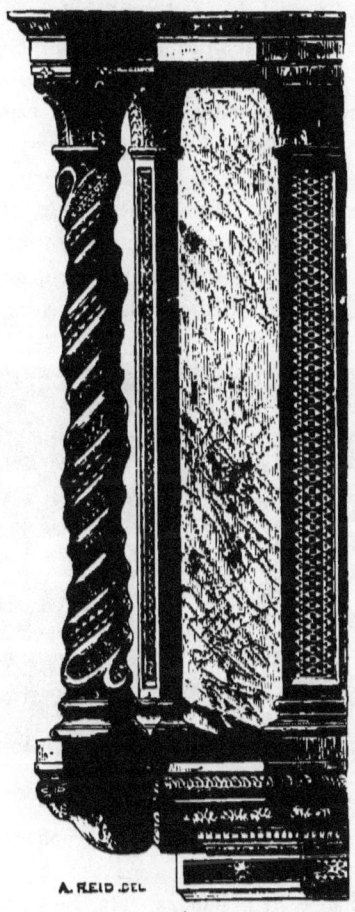

A. REID DEL.
In the church of Ara Cœli, at Rome.

Italy; but we may boast of one or two in our own country. The shrine of Edward the confessor in Westminster abbey, which was finished under Henry the third, bears an inscription recording it to have been executed in the year 1270. The tomb also exhibits some very beautiful pieces of the same process, but in a wretched state of dilapidation.

A third variety of Christian and mediæval mosaic, commonly used for the paving of Italian churches from the fourth or fifth century down to the thirteenth, is called the *Opus Alexandrinum*. It may be described, generally, as tesselated marble work; an arrangement of small cubes, usually of porphyry or serpentine, composing geometrical patterns in grooves, cut in the white marble slabs which form the pavement. We have reason to believe that this variety did not remain in general use nearly so late as either of the two previously described, and that it was discontinued about the end of the thirteenth century.

From Monreale.

The employment of mosaic was not confined to Europe but obtained during the middle ages to a very considerable extent among eastern nations. In India, at Agra and

Delhi, in the form of inlaying with precious stones, marbles, and coloured compositions; in Turkey and Asia minor large pieces of *faience*, coloured on the surface, were fitted together. In Spain, the Moors adopted it as an essential element for decorating walls: one instance only occurs in the Alhambra of mosaic employed for pavement.

There was an interval of two or three hundred years, during which the use of mosaic gradually died out in Italy and other European countries and the excellence of its manufacture of course declined also; but mosaic was too congenial to Italian taste to remain long in obscurity. With the revival of learning in the sixteenth century attention was naturally directed to the restoration of some of the ancient processes. The decoration of the domes of St. Peter's, about the year 1600, created a great demand at Rome for workmen in mosaic and a regular school was established, now called the "Fabrica." The well-known copy of Guido's St. Michael, in one of the chapels of St. Peter's, was executed in 1644 by Giovanni Callandra.

The modern process of making mosaics now commonly followed at Rome is this:—a plate, generally of metal, of the required size is first surrounded by a margin rising about three quarters of an inch from the surface. A mastic cement, composed of powdered stone, lime, and linseed oil, is then spread over as a coating, perhaps a quarter of an inch in thickness. When set, this is again covered with plaster of Paris rising to a level with the margin; upon which is traced a very careful outline of the picture to be copied, and just so much as will admit of the insertion of the small pieces of *smalto* or glass is removed from time to time with a fine chisel. The workman then selects from the trays, in which are kept thousands of varieties of colour, a piece of the tint which he wants and carefully brings it to the necessary shape. The piece is then moistened with a little cement and bedded in its proper situation:—the process being repeated until the picture is finished;—

when the whole, being ground down to an even face and polished, becomes an imperishable work of art. The process is the same for making the small mosaics so much employed at the present day for boxes, covers, or articles of jewellery; and this work is sometimes upon almost a microscopic scale.

The Florentine mosaic which is chiefly used for the decoration of altars and tombs, or for cabinets, tops of tables, coffers and the like, is composed of precious materials in small slices or veneers: and by taking advantage of the natural tints and shades which characterise the marble, the agate or the jasper, very admirable effects may be produced in imitation of fruit, flowers, or ornaments. The use of this kind of mosaic is extremely restricted, on account of the great value and expense not only of the materials but of the labour which is spent upon them. None but the hardest stones are used; every separate piece must be backed by thicker slices of slate or marble to obtain additional strength; and every minute portion must be ground until it exactly corresponds with the pattern previously cut.

Indian mosaic; from the Taj Mahal.

ARMS AND ARMOUR.

Mounted knight, from seal of Duke of Burgundy; fourteenth century.

M.

ARMS AND ARMOUR.

EAPONS of defence and offence are, and must have been, among the very earliest things made: nor is it necessary to attribute this fact (as some have) to the evil passions of humanity. To obtain food from slain animals of the field and forest and to defend himself from the attacks of ferocious animals were the first necessities of primeval man. Hence, in almost every deposit where prehistoric remains are buried we find clubs, hatchets, arrows or the like. Nor are these always rude in manufacture; ornament of some kind seems to have been coeval with protection; and the celt and hammer head of even the stone age often assume graceful outlines, not essential to the practical purpose for which the weapon was made.

Leaving these mysterious ages, and passing over (it may be) thousands of years, historic records prove the care and labour spent upon the decoration of arms and armour from the first periods of the Egyptian, Assyrian, and Greek peoples. The painted tombs at Thebes and the sculptured walls of the palaces at Nineveh have supplied us with many examples of armour and weapons, reaching back to the fifth or sixth Egyptian dynasty, before the exodus of the Israelites. Classical Greek authors, and especially the poets, from the days of Hesiod and Homer are full of notices and allusions. The golden armour of Glaucus, the shield of Agamemnon, and the wondrous armour of Achilles, although perhaps poetically to some degree imagined, must have been described from real types and examples which Homer had himself seen. Nor are we left, scarcely a century or two later, merely to poetical descriptions from which we may learn what ancient armour and the ornaments of it were. Besides the information which we derive from vases and bas-reliefs various fragments have been found in Greek and Etruscan tombs, clearly showing the artistic and beautiful decoration which was bestowed on armour. Once, when a tomb in Etruria was opened the buried chieftain was seen clothed in full armour, and resting on a couch of bronze: and although the skeleton quickly mouldered into dust, and much of the iron perished also on exposure to the air, enough was left and especially of the rich gold ornaments to enable us to form a complete idea of the living warrior. Two small portions of the shoulder pieces of a bronze Greek breastplate are in the British museum; and it is hardly possible to conceive any art or workmanship more admirable than that which first designed and then executed the figures which decorate these pieces in high relief.

The student will find ample information upon the arms and accoutrements of the Greeks, and of the Romans in imperial times, in the numerous books which treat of classical literature: it is needful here only to say with regret that existing examples, even of the smaller arms, are of the greatest rarity. Much can be learnt also from engravings of the sculptures on the triumphal arches at Rome, or from the column of Trajan; not only as to the equipments of the Roman soldier but of other European nations in Roman pay, the German, the Dacian, and the Goth.

Mounted barbarian in the Roman service; from a bas-relief.

In England, from time to time, a few swords and daggers and shields and spear heads have been found, varying in date from the Roman occupation to the time of the Norman conqueror. Portions also of horse trappings and buckles of girdles or the like are also to be seen in many collections; and these are the more valuable, as showing the style of ornament among the British, Saxon, and Danish inhabitants of our island. Shields were enriched with ornaments in low relief, and the smaller weapons often with enamel also. We must attribute the rarity of extant specimens to the perishable nature of the body armour of the Saxons and Danes and of the early Norman invaders: it was principally composed of rings or small plates, stitched upon leather or stout linen, which would soon decay. A very interesting discovery was also, some years ago, made at Hallstadt, in Austria; where bronze and iron weapons, many of them long swords, were found lying close by gold ornaments: these are preserved at Vienna.

We have a few evidences of what the Carlovingian weapons were and their style of ornament in the manuscripts and ivory carvings of the ninth and tenth centuries, and some small remains have been found in graves in France. About the end of the eleventh we can refer to the Bayeux tapestry, which gives us many representations of the arms and armour both of the Norman and of the English at that time, by the hand certainly of a contemporary and possibly of an eye-witness of many of the scenes. Here we see the Conqueror himself in a complete suit of mail, others in scale armour, some with their legs protected by bands only; the helmets are conical with a bar to protect the face, and the shields pointed or kite shape. The weapons are axes, swords, and bows. The shields seem to be ornamented, but we can scarcely say with any heraldic device. It is not until the middle of the

Norman archer, from Bayeux tapestry.

twelfth century that we can find distinct evidence of such decoration, and in England at least we believe that no heralds' roll exists of an earlier date than 1240. A sword, incorrectly ascribed to Hugh Lupus, the first earl of Chester, is in the British museum. The handle is enriched with pieces of mother-of-pearl, and the pommel presents some good chasing. Another mediæval sword in the same collection has enamelled coats of arms on the handle.

From about this time, 1200, we can refer to numerous illustrations upon monuments and brasses, on ivory carvings, and in the illuminated manuscripts which tell us with sufficient exactness the general form and the usual style of ornament of arms and armour. We can see therefore, from this instance only, how

From a manuscript of the thirteenth century.

valuable for other purposes than mere works of art in themselves, are contemporary records of any kind. They enable us to trace the varying fashions and the improvements which were required as age after age passed by. But we still have only one or two extant examples either of arms or armour of the early mediæval period. Four or five helmets, in different conditions of injury, have been discovered; one, of the time of king John, was exhibited at Manchester in 1857. The helmet, a shield, and the gaunt-

Mounted knight, twelfth century; from a seal.

lets of the Black Prince are yet preserved in Canterbury cathedral. Some years back his sword and another shield were there also, but cathedral custodians were then—it is to be hoped are not so now—both careless and ignorant, and these have disappeared. The dean and chapter of Hereford a little while ago gave (what was not theirs to give) the jousting helmet of Sir Richard Pembridge who died in 1475, which was suspended over his tomb under their charge, to Sir Samuel Meyrick; who can tell where this is now, since the dispersion of the Meyrick collection? The tilting helmet, saddle, and shield of Henry the fifth are in Westminster abbey. Some complete suits of armour of

Helmet of the thirteenth century.

the middle of the fifteenth century may be seen in the Tower and in a few other great collections.

Armour of the fifteenth century.

The full suit of armour, entirely of plate iron, was not known until about the year 1300. It was first worn in Italy, but not adopted in France and England for some years later. With its introduction came the opportunity also of much decoration. At first, this consisted chiefly of flutings, hammered out; with the addition sometimes of other ornaments. But before the reign of Henry the eighth far greater labour and much higher artistic decoration were applied to armour. The helmet and every other part were covered with embossed figures or arabesques, engraved, chased, and damascened with gold and silver; the shields and sword hilts especially were often carved with very complicated subjects in bas-relief. The richest armour was executed in Italy; but there were also artists of renown in Germany, particularly at Augsburg, and in France.

Tournament helmet; fifteenth century.

The decoration of armour, on breastplates, shields, and other large pieces, was usually executed in hammer, or repoussé, work. This consisted in beating out the sheet of metal with a hammer, so as to express upon the surface the proposed design in relief. Although much lightness may be given to cast metal by means of the perfection of the mould, it can never be compared with that of a sheet of metal reduced to the required thinness by the hammer, nor can the design be so freely and finely executed as by the hand.

Ancient cannon in the Tower.

When fire-arms became more common and portable in shape, they were equally fitting subjects for art decoration. The barrels of the arquebuses and pistols were enriched with chasings, or were damascened: and the stock was inlaid with ivory or stained wood, and the subjects elaborately and delicately engraved. So, again,

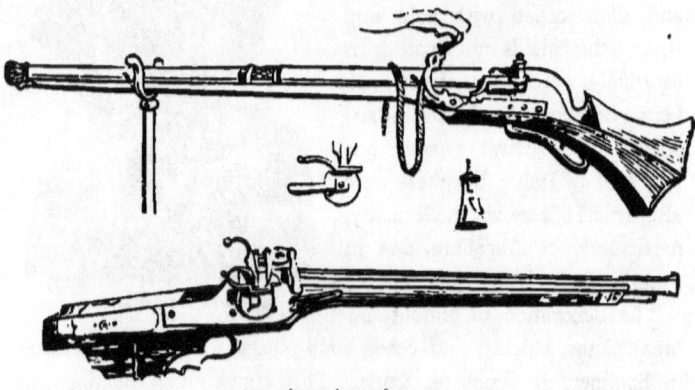

Arquebus; sixteenth century.

the powder flasks, of which many good examples excellent both in design and workmanship are to be found in almost every collection. Cannon and other fire-arms did not supersede the old weapon, the bow and arrow, for many years after their invention: so slowly indeed that we find a company of the once famous English archers assisting at the siege of Rochelle in 1627: this is probably the last instance of their employment in action which can be referred to. Specimens of the mediæval long bow are of the utmost rarity: the material was perishable and there was little to induce people to preserve them when their use in warfare or in hunting had altogether ceased. On the other hand many cross-bows still exist: and the same kind of rich decoration, especially in inlaid ivory with carved or engraved subjects, is often to be found upon both the handle and the bow.

No weapons ever made in Europe excelled even if any equalled

ARMS AND ARMOUR. 237

the swords and daggers of oriental nations and especially of India. The people of those countries may be said to have endowed violence and cruelty with the utmost grace. As regards perfection of workmanship, their daggers with short, sharp pointed, cutting blades make deadly wounds hardly drawing a single drop of blood or scarcely leaving a visible trace. As regards ornaments, the handles not only of their swords and daggers but of maces, spears, and battle-axes are covered with gold and precious stones, rubies, and sapphires and diamonds. One example of a dagger which was a few years ago in a French collection offered a very singular illusion of blood in its costly decoration; a hollow line is engraved upon the steel blade, the sides of which form a frame for a number of small rubies, so that when the weapon is flourished the jewels glitter like drops of blood, fresh and limpid. All, in fact, seems perfect in oriental armour and weapons:—the intense degree of sharpness which renders it credible that a filmy gauze scarf can be cut in two by the stroke of a scimitar; the ornamentation so exquisitely damascened or nielloed that it looks like delicate lace; coats of mail fine and light almost as a linen robe; helmets which are little more than skull caps, amply protecting the head but leaving it all its natural shape; the shield small and round so as not to interfere with the action of the wearer; and, lastly, the graceful outline of the sword, in form like the crescent moon, the symbol of the creed itself of the eastern warrior.

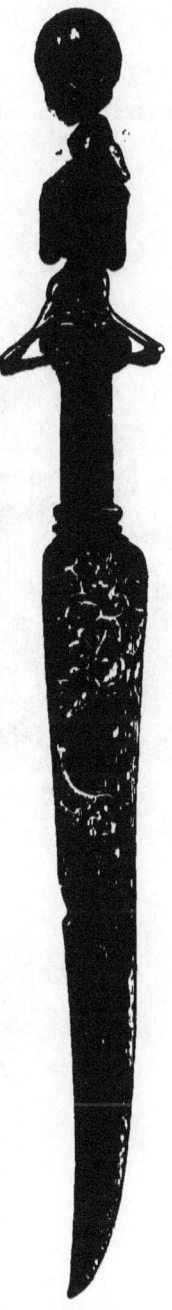

Moorish dagger, fifteenth century.

238 *ARMS AND ARMOUR.*

There are some very interesting and good examples of modern oriental arms in the South Kensington museum.

Knights, in complete armour, about 1500.

TEXTILES.

Ladies spinning and weaving; from a manuscript of the fifteenth century.

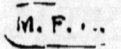

TEXTILES.

HE word "textile" means every kind of stuff wrought in the loom: hence, whether the threads be spun from the produce of the animal, vegetable, or mineral kingdom, whether of sheep's wool, goats' hair, camels' wool, or camels' hair; whether of flax, hemp, mallow, or the filaments drawn out of the leaves of plants of the lily and asphodel tribes of flowers, or the fibrous coating about pods, or cotton; whether of gold, silver, or of any other metal; the webs from all such materials are textiles. Unlike these are other appliances for garment-making in many countries; and of such not the least curious, perhaps odd to our ideas, is paper, which is much employed for the purpose by the Japanese. A careful reference to a map will show us the materials which from the earliest ages the inhabitants of the world had at hand, in every clime, for making articles of dress, and, probably, also for other textiles.

In cold countries the furred skins of various animals could easily, even with no other help than a thorn or piece of bone for a needle, be fashioned into the necessary clothing. At the first beginning and in most countries sheep, probably, were bred more for raiment than for food. Before shearing was invented the locks of wool were torn away by the hand, and from the earliest known time spun by women from a distaff. This was not a mere employment of the lower classes, but in many lands and especially among Anglo-saxon women was a work practised by all ranks, from the king's daughter downwards. We have numerous proofs of this in old English records; the term "spinster" is derived from an occupation so common, and the name of spindle tree is still given to a plant found almost everywhere in England on account of the good spindles made from its wood.

Woollen stuffs were originally not woven but plaited by the older inhabitants of Britain; and bodies have been found in graves, so wrapt up. As years passed on the loom was introduced, fashioned after the simplest form. Dion Cassius, who wrote in the second century, tells us that Boadicea wore under her cloak a motley tunic, checquered with many colours. This garment was, possibly, a native stuff woven of worsted in a pattern like the modern Scotch plaids.

The home of cotton is in the east: and the various peoples of those lands, time out of mind, have clothed themselves in fabrics made of cotton, gathered from a plant of the mallow tribe, which grew wild there. Hemp is a plant of the nettle tribe, common in the north of Europe. More than two thousand years ago Herodotus speaks of it as cultivated in Scythia. "The Thracians" he says "make clothing of it like linen, nor can one easily distinguish between cloths of hemp or flax." The Latin name is "cannabis;" whence we have taken our own word canvas, meaning any texture woven of hempen thread.

Flax grows wild in very many countries, but we must once more turn to the Egyptians for the earliest examples of fine flaxen textiles: and so famous were they that their own word "byssus" was the term among Greeks and Romans for linen. The plague of hail was sent when "the flax was bolled;" and hundreds of years afterwards Solomon praises "the fine linen" of Egypt, and the prophets warn that land that "they shall be confounded who comb and weave fine linen." We have, moreover, existing proofs of the excellence of their workmanship; many mummies have been found rolled up in bandages of linen which fully bear out the praises anciently bestowed upon the beauty of Egyptian loom-work. Pieces are in the British museum which appear to be made, according to Sir G. Wilkinson, "of yarns of nearly 100 hanks in the pound, with 140 threads in an inch in the warp and 64 in the woof."

The history of silk is curious and interesting: it was unknown to the old Egyptians, nor is there evidence that any one of the most ancient nations of the world knew of it, either as a simple twist or as a woven stuff. Although the word "silk" occurs in one or two places of the English version of the Old Testament, the best authorities agree that the original is wrongly translated; and we can find no mention of it before the time of Aristotle. The manufacture and the use of silk spread rapidly in the west after its introduction from China and India, whence undoubtedly it came. About the reign of Augustus silks for robes were made of

Indian woman reeling silk from a wheel.

so thin a texture, that they showed rather than concealed the limbs; and both poets and moralists were loud in their condemnation of garments " which were a protection neither for the body nor from shame."

It is far from improbable that the small shreds of very delicate and transparent silk, sometimes found between the leaves of ancient manuscripts, might be relics of silks of this kind, preserved from the classic period. They occur, it may be remembered, in the manuscript of Theodulph, now at Puy de Velay.

Although silk was worn by the Romans under the empire the cost of it was excessively high, and few could afford such robes; at first also they were looked on as unbecoming for men's wear, and were forbidden. On extraordinary occasions exception was allowed; as when Titus and Vespasian wore such dresses in celebrating their triumph. Aurelian refused to allow his wife a mantle of purple silk on account of the extravagant value; a pound of gold was the price of a pound of silk.

Clothing however, made either wholly or in part of silk, gradually became more and more sought for, and Byzantium was renowned for the beauty of its stuffs. Still, the raw silk had to be brought from the east; until two Greek monks who had lived among the Chinese learned the whole process of rearing the worm. Returning home, they carried with them a number of eggs hidden in their staffs and these were hatched at Constantinople. Soon afterwards the western world produced its own silk, and southern Italy especially wrought very rich stuffs.

In spreading westward silks retained the names by which they were commonly known in Greece, or Asia minor, or Persia. Hence, when we read of samit, cendal, baudekin, and other names which have long been dropt by the trade, we should bear in mind that under a wide variety of spelling these names guide us to the country where the particular kind was originally made.

Various materials besides wool, cotton, and silk have been from the earliest ages used for weaving; more particularly gold, which judiciously employed adds not barbaric but artistical richness. The Egyptians produced splendid garments of gold mixed with linen, long before the days of Moses; sometimes also gold alone was woven: but in either case the metal was cut into very narrow, thin, flat slips, and never worked in a round or wire shape. The modern Chinese and people of India still work the gold into their stuffs after the ancient form.

It is clear from Homer and other poets that the Grecian women were skilled workers of ornamental clothing. Penelope is described as throwing over Ulysses an upper garment, richly decorated. The tunic of the Greeks was frequently adorned with sprigs, spots, stripes or other devices, and with borders of an elaborate pattern.

The old historians, Greek and Roman, frequently tell us of the superb dresses of purple and gold worn by great personages in the east; and the same fashion rapidly extended to Rome, long before the beginning of the empire. Pliny speaks of gold cloth as well known and that it might be woven like wool, alone or mixed with it. In a very ancient grave, opened in 1840, the body of a Roman lady was found with fragments of the robe in which she had been buried, made of fine flat gold threads. Coming to Christian times we have the evidence of the body of St Cecilia, martyred in the year 230, which was seen dressed, when her tomb was opened, in a garment all of gold. Many such examples might be cited; we can now name only the burial cloak in which Childeric, who died A.D. 485, was found wrapt up; and the pieces of Anglo-saxon vestments preserved in the cathedral library at Durham. After the eleventh century, royal robes and church vestments of cloth of gold are mentioned over and over again in records and wills and inventories.

Cloths of gold were not all alike; some looked (as it were) dead; others, brilliant and sparkling. When the gold is twisted into its silken filament it appears dull; when the flattened strip is rolled about so evenly as to bring the edges close, it seems to be one unbroken lustrous wire of gold, like that we now call "passing," and rich silks so woven during the middle ages were known as damasks of Cyprus. About the beginning of the fifteenth century this bright shimmering golden textile, worn generally on solemn occasions or at royal ceremonials, was named "tissue;" and the thin smooth paper, first made to be put between the folds of a stuff so delicate, yet keeps, though the original use is forgotten, the name of tissue-paper.

It is unnecessary to observe more than the mere fact that silver was wrought and woven, cut into long narrow shreds, like gold.

At what distant period these slips of gold and silver were drawn into long, round, hair-like threads or wire is not known. Very ancient fragments, looking like wire, have been found at Thebes: but these may have been doubled and rubbed by the fingers, or between pieces of polished stone. The first wire-drawing machine was invented (as some assert) about 1360, at Nuremberg, but it was not brought to England until 1560. There are two early examples of this pure wire, woven with silk, at South Kensington; no. 8581, and no. 8228. The practice of twining the strips of gold or silver round a line of silk or flax may be traced far back.

Silks in mediæval times had various names, distinguishing either their quality, or their pattern, or whence they came. *Holosericum* was stuff made entirely of silk; *subsericum*, partly so *Examitum*, or as our old English documents so often call it, *samit*, tells (from the Greek *ἑξ*, for six) the number of threads in the warp of the texture. To say, therefore, that any robe was of "samit" meant that it was six-threaded, and costly and splendid. When Sir Launcelot came to king Arthur, the old poet writes:

> "Launcelot and the queen were clede
> In robes of a riche wede,
> Of samit white, with silver shredde."

The strong modern silks with the thick thread "organzine" for the woof, and a slightly thinner thread "tram" for the warp, may be regarded as representing the old samits.

TEXTILES. 247

As rich as the samit was cyclatoun, so called from the Persian name which came westward with it, meaning bright and glittering; but unlike the samit this was light in texture, thin and glossy. Frequently a golden thread lent still more glitter, and cyclatoun was much used both for ecclesiastical vestments and for ceremonial dress. The woodcut shows the embroidered mitre,

Embroidered vestments of the twelfth century.

chasuble, and stole, said to have belonged to St. Thomas à Becket, A.D. 1170.

Even thinner in texture though less costly was another silken stuff, often mentioned in mediæval books and documents: namely, *cendal* or *syndon;* of which the last kind was the least rich, and commonly used as a lining for vestments and cloaks. *Taffeta* although still made of silk was, again, less costly than either cendal or syndon.

Sarcenet, in the fifteenth century, took by degrees in England the place of cendal, in consequence of some improvement which was made in the manufacture by the Saracens, probably in Spain. It was soon much sought after, and from the markets whence it came was at first called " saracenicum : " but it quickly had the name by which we still know it, sarcenet. *Satin*, though not so common as other silken textures, was worn in England in the middle ages; and Chaucer tells us that the company of Surrey chapmen sold " satins riche of hewe." Originally, along the shores of the Mediterranean these silks were called " aceytuni," then shortened by Italians into " zetani," and smoothed by French and English into satin. The earliest mention which we have found of this term is among the gifts of bishop Grandison to Exeter cathedral about 1350. *Carda* or *carduus* was another kind of silk, of inferior quality, chiefly used for hangings and curtains. We find mention also in old inventories of *camoca*, both for church vestments and for daily dress; and of *cloth of Tars*; which last may possibly have been not silk but fine wool from Thibet, the forerunner of our modern cashmere.

We do not know when *velvet* was first woven or the people who hit upon the mode of making it; probably, first in China, and in Europe in the south of Spain or Italy. The oldest piece which can be referred to is a crimson cope of the fourteenth century, still preserved at the Catholic college of Mount St. Mary, Chesterfield.

The name itself "velluto" seems to point out Italy as the

market through which it was first obtained. *Fustian* was used before the year 1300: St. Paul's cathedral then had a cope of this material; it was not thought much of, and an old English sermon blames a priest who had his chasuble made "of medeme fustian." But it is not improbable that the hint of making velvets from silk was given by the manufacture of fustian from cotton: and being once known, improvements rapidly followed. Especially velvet was diapered, and the pattern, upon a ground of silk or gold, came out boldly and richly. Several sorts are included in old documents; velvets "plain"; "raised," and "purshed," that is, raised in a network pattern.

The term *diaper* was itself given to a silken fabric, greatly estimated in England and abroad for many centuries. As early as 1066, a diaper chasuble of cloth of gold was given to the monastery of Monte Casino: and soon after we have notices in English inventories of red and white diapers.

We find no description of stuff oftener spoken of by mediæval writers and in records than *baudekin*, a rich silk, shot with gold or other coloured silks, brought first from Bagdad or Baldak. Cloths of gold so tinted were soon commonly known as "baldakin" or "baudekin"; and no material was more worn upon state occasions by great personages. Henry the third had such a robe in the year 1247, when he knighted William of Valence; ten or twelve years later copes are said to have been made of baudekin; and we have frequent mention of it afterwards.

Muslin, from the earliest antiquity, has been the favourite material both for dress and furniture in the greater part of Asia. Not only were its charms derived from a cloud-like lightness and delicacy, but from stripes of gold tastefully woven in the warp. The cotton plant grew everywhere in those regions, and Mosul (which stands near the site of Nineveh) was celebrated above other Asiatic cities for the peculiar beauty of its fabrics, and from that place we still give the name of muslin to this beautiful cotton web.

250   TEXTILES.

The fine collection of textiles at South Kensington will tell the student how to distribute old examples into various schools, and so enable him to arrive at some classification of the countries which were the first seats of the different manufactures. *Chinese* fabrics are easily distinguished; and very probably the lapse of a thousand years has produced but slight alterations either in their style or substance. A writer upon geography, who lived before the end of the second century, says that the Chinese make "precious figured garments, resembling in colour the flowers of the field, and rivalling in fineness the work of spiders." *Persian* textiles

Silk damask (Sicilian) with imitated Arabic letters: fifteenth century.

also are very ancient, and easily known by their type of ornament. *Byzantine* and other oriental silks and cottons are distinguished by characteristic patterns; various adaptations of the Christian symbol, the cross, abound upon the one; and beasts, birds, and the eastern "tree of life" upon Syrian and Arabic stuffs. *Saracenic* work often has longitudinal stripes of blue or red or other colours, and imitations of letters woven into the pattern, as if a sentence from the Koran or in praise of the monarch for whom the web was woven. These different oriental styles are to be traced in the earlier productions of Sicily and Italy; where, at

Silk damask—Florentine: fifteenth century.

Palermo, Genoa, Lucca, Florence, and Venice, the manufactures soon obtained a wide sale, and the looms supplied silks and velvets to the whole of western Europe.

TEXTILES.

We have already spoken of the woollen stuffs made in Britain in very early times; and in later ages, from the twelfth century downwards, English work was famous, not in that class only but for linens. Worcester, Norwich, and Bath were celebrated and successful above the others; and a stuff of such high quality was made from wool carded at Worstead in Norfolk that the name of the town was given to it. Exeter cathedral in the fourteenth century had vestments "of black worsted;" and we find bequeathed in wills of the same period beds "of red worsted embroidered" and "cushions of my best red worsted." Irish cloth, white and red, was used in England in the reign of king John; and among the accounts of a bishop of Hereford in 1290 is a payment for Irish cloth for linings. Flemish textiles were greatly esteemed during the middle ages; and Matthew of Westminster praises the

The weaver; sixteenth century; from the engraving by J. Amman.

rich garments which we obtained from Flanders in return for the material, namely, wool, which England sent her. So large was the trade in these things between the two countries in the reign of Edward the third that very important political events depended

Part of the orphrey of the Syon cope.

upon its not being interrupted. English embroidery was much sought after: the woodcut (p. 13) represents a portion of the famous "Syon cope," now at South Kensington.

Tapestry is neither real weaving nor true embroidery. Though wrought upon a loom and upon a warp stretched out along its frame there is no woof thrown across the threads with a shuttle, but the weft is worked with many short threads of various colours, put in with a needle. Tapestry runs back into remote antiquity. The woman in the Proverbs says, "I have covered my bed with painted tapestry, brought from Egypt." The Greeks and Romans used tapestry for curtains and other hangings; and the employment of it for like purposes was common throughout Europe in succeeding ages. Old English records are full of references to

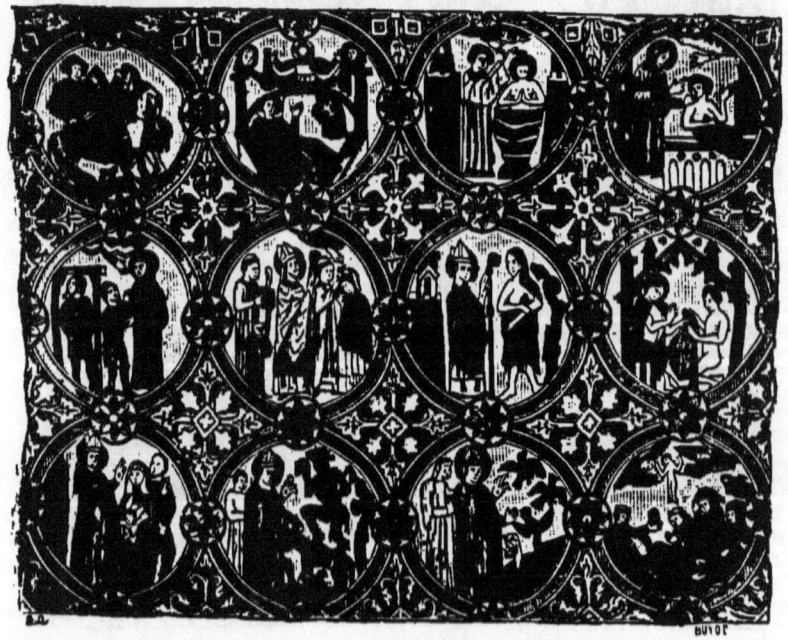

The Legend of St. Martin.—From a piece of tapestry of the fourteenth century in the Louvre.

and descriptions of tapestry. A few remarkable pieces still exist, particularly a large example at St. Mary's hall, Coventry, representing the marriage of Henry the sixth; and a fine piece in a private house in Cornwall, the marriage of Henry the seventh. Arras was the usual name for hangings of this kind, owing to the excellence of the work produced in that town.

French tapestry has long been famous also. Francis the first brought Flemish workmen to Fontainebleau and the establishment was kept up by his successors. A hundred years later, Colbert, the celebrated minister of Louis the fourteenth, took under his protection a manufactory which had been set up by two brothers, of the name of Gobelin, originally dyers: and, in a very short time, the productions of the Hôtel royal des Gobelins were universally admired. The well-known tapestries which for many generations hung upon the walls of the House of Lords were destroyed in the fire of 1834: these were Flemish, and executed in the reign of queen Elizabeth to commemorate the destruction of the Spanish armada. But, probably, the culminating point in the history of tapestry was when Raffaelle was employed to make designs for a series of Scripture subjects, to be hung upon the walls of the Sistine chapel in Rome. They are now in the Vatican; in a dilapidated state (and one has perished), having been more than once removed from Rome. Seven of the original cartoons exist in England; and belong to the crown. For some years past they have been lent to the museum at South Kensington.

Charles the first purchased these cartoons, and copies in tapestry of four or five of them were made at Mortlake, where were some tapestry works in which he took a great interest. This Mortlake establishment fell into decay about the end of the seventeenth century, since which time no attempt seems to have been tried in England to apply this costly manufacture to any other purpose than to produce carpets and similar articles.

Carpets are akin to tapestry, and though the use of them may not be so ancient yet is very old. Mediæval examples are rare; and the student may be recommended to examine carefully two pieces, fortunately, in the collection at South Kensington, no. 8649, of the fourteenth century, and no. 8357, of the sixteenth; both of Spanish work. Before the introduction of carpets, the chambers in houses and in royal palaces and the chancels of our parish churches were strewed with rushes.

Embroidered hangings of a bed; from a MS. of the fifteenth century.

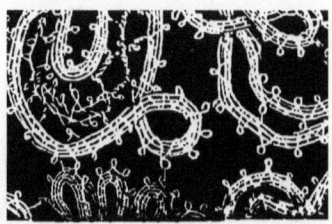

Guipure Lace; Italian, seventeenth century.

M.F.A.

LACE.

NO textile fabric has contributed more largely to the elegancies and luxuries of life than lace, the most delicate of all. The earliest and most splendid specimens were produced in convents, works of such exquisite skill and patient toil as could only have been executed by those to whom it was a labour of love, and whose dearest office was to deck with the choicest productions of their needle the shrine of their favourite saint. When lace passed into more general use, it was worn in the greatest profusion. Lace attends us on every special occasion of life. It envelopes the infant at the baptismal font, veils the bride at the altar, and still enshrouds the dead in many countries of southern Europe.

The first lace made was of heavy texture, adapted to the solid materials that formed the costume of the period. It partook more of the character of embroidery, with which it was then constantly united; and consisted of two descriptions called "lacis" or "darned netting," and "cutwork."

Lacis was a network of square ground, called "Rézeuil," upon which the pattern was either darned or worked in with counted stitches, "Point compté," like the modern "Filet brodé;" or formed of pieces of linen cut out and sewn on or "applied" to the net. This kind of work was executed in large pieces for altar cloths, coverlets, the borders of curtains, and bed hangings, and was often worked in coloured silks and gold thread. It is also called "Opus araneum," or "spiderwork."

Cutwork was made in different manners. A network of threads was attached or gummed to a piece of cloth called quintin, from the town in Brittany where it was first fabricated, and the pattern formed by sewing round the parts of the cloth that were to remain with button-hole stitch, and cutting the rest away; hence the name of cutwork. At other times no cloth was used, but the threads were arranged on a frame radiating from a common centre, and then worked into various patterns, formed throughout by variations of two stitches, as here shown.

To this class belong the old conventual lace of Italy, often called "Greek lace," and the finer and more delicate geometric laces which in the 16th and 17th centuries were in universal use, and were all comprised under the general name of "cutworks." Embroidery, lacis, and cutwork are often combined in the same piece, squares of lacis alternating with squares of linen, in which both embroidery and cutwork are introduced. Many examples are in the museum, among the altar cloths and other objects of ecclesiastical use, of fine and most curious workmanship.

In the 16th century the making of lacis and cutwork formed the principal occupation of the ladies of the day, and numerous books of patterns were published for their use; most of them were printed in Italy. Among these, the work of Frederick Vinciolo, a Venetian, was most widely circulated. These books have now become scarce.

Lace is made of gold, silver, silk, cotton, and flax, to which may be added poil-de-chèvre, and also the fibre of the aloe, employed by the peasants near Genoa and in Spain. It consists of two parts, the ground (*French* réseau) and the pattern. The ground is generally a plain network of honeycomb or six-sided meshes, variously formed in the different kinds of lace; and in some of the older descriptions, instead of the network ground, the pattern or flowers are connected by irregular threads overcast with button-hole stitch, or fringed with loops or knots, also styled "thorns." In some kinds of lace there is no ground at all, the flowers joining each other. The pattern or flower, technically called "gimp" or "cloth," from its compact texture, is either made together with the ground, as in Mechlin, Valenciennes, and Buckingham; or separately, as in Brussels or Honiton, where it is afterwards either worked into the ground or sewn on, "applied." The little raised cord which surrounds the pattern is called "cordonnet." Lace has two edges; the upper, called "pearl" or "picot," consists of a row of little points at equal distances, forming a kind of fringe to the edge; and the lower or "footing," a narrow lace that serves to strengthen the ground and to sew the lace to the material upon which it is to be worn. The openwork or fancy stitches are termed "fillings" or "modes."

Lace is divided into two classes, point and pillow. Point is made with a needle on a parchment pattern; pillow by the weaving, twisting, and plaiting of the threads with bobbins, upon the well known cushion which bears its name.

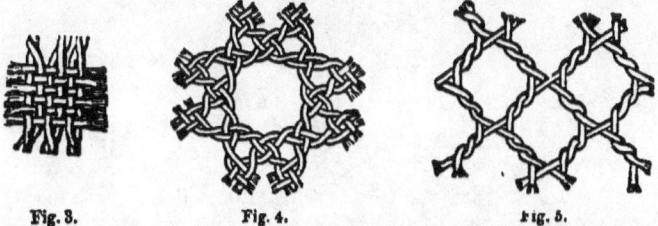

Fig. 3. Fig. 4. Fig. 5.

The pattern in most of the varieties is made by weaving or "clothing" (fig. 3); the ground or mesh by plaiting (fig. 4); or in other varieties, by twisting the threads (fig. 5). Fig. 4 represents the four-thread Brussels or Honiton ground.

The principal point (*i.e.* strictly, needle-made) laces are the ancient laces of Italy, Spain, and Portugal; and the more modern lace of France, called point d'Alençon. The pillow laces are those of Mechlin, Lille, Valenciennes, Honiton, Buckingham, and many manufactories in France. Brussels makes both point and pillow.

The Italians claim the invention of needle-made lace from a very early period, but it was not until the 16th century that it came into universal use; and the points or cutworks of Italy were, with those of Flanders, in general request to form the ruff of queen Elizabeth, the falling collar of Charles the first, and the "Whisk" or Medicean ruff of his queen Henrietta Maria. Lace was then worn in the greatest extravagance at the courts of England and France, and not only were the ruffs, cuffs, caps, collars, handkerchiefs, and aprons of lace, but even the tops of the boots were trimmed with the same costly material. In under clothing the linen breadths were united by a narrow insertion called "Seaming" lace, and sheets, pillow cases, and bed curtains were joined in the same manner. All the lace of this period is of geometric design, in squares or circles variously combined.

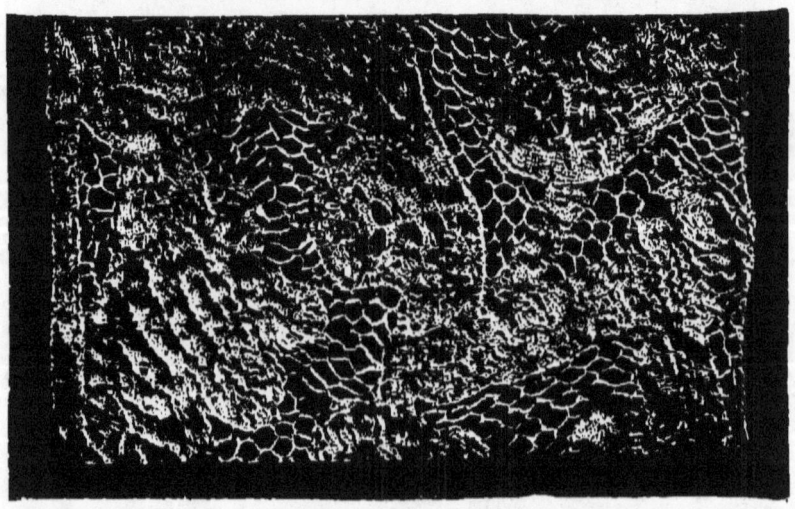

Ancient Point, Italian, seventeenth century.

It is not until the end of the 17th century that these forms are replaced by the flowing lines of the Louis XIV. style. Lace, like every other ornamental fabric, partakes of the character of the time.

In examining Italian and Spanish lace of the 16th and 17th centuries, it is to be borne in mind that though the finer needle points belong to Italy and especially to Venice; the points in

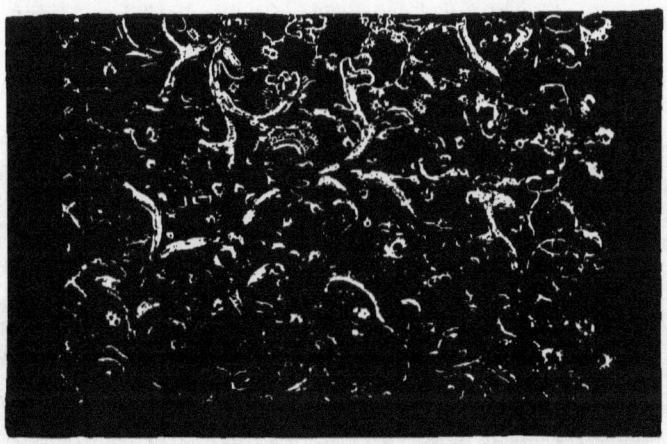

Finest raised Venetian Point; seventeenth century.

relief to Venice and Spain; and those made on the pillow to Genoa; yet, as all were the produce of the convent or of private industry, though a general national characteristic may be assigned to each, the same laces may have been made in almost every country of Europe.

If Italy claims the priority of needle-made lace, it is to the Netherlands that we must assign, at a very early period, the invention of the pillow. Lace-making has ever been one of the chief industries of that country, and one of the great sources of its national wealth. When every other manufacture was extinguished by the religious persecutions of the sixteenth century, the lace trade alone upheld itself and saved the country from ruin. There are now nearly a thousand schools in Belgium devoted to this teaching, where the children at a very early age learn to twist the bobbins with wonderful dexterity. The old Flemish lace is of great beauty, and the "cutworks" and "points of Flanders" were, in the 16th century, equally esteemed with those of Italy. The laces of Brussels and Mechlin alone were distinguished later by their special names; all other fabrics of the Netherlands were known under the general designation of "Flanders" lace. That description in which the flowers join or are united by "brides," usually called guipure, was in general use for the lace cravats of

Guipure, Flemish, seventeenth century.

the 17th century, and the bold flowing scroll patterns are in the purest style of Louis XIV.

Most celebrated of all manufactures of lace is that of Brussels, distinguished for the beauty of its ground, the perfection of its flowers, and the elegance of its patterns. The thread is of extraordinary fineness, made of the flax of Brabant. It is spun underground, for contact with the air causes it to break, being so fine as almost to escape the sight,—the lace spinner is guided only by touch. Hand-spun thread costs sometimes as high as 240*l*. the lb., and is consequently now but little used, a Scotch cotton thread being substituted, except for the finest lace; but machine-made thread has never arrived at the fineness of that made by hand.

The ground used in Brussels lace is of two kinds, needle-point, "point à l'aiguille," and pillow. The needle-point is made in small segments of an inch wide, and united by the invisible stitch called "fine joining." It is stronger, but three times more expensive than the pillow, and is rarely used except for royal orders. In the pillow-made ground two sides of the hexagonal mesh are

Lappet, Brussels; eighteenth century.

formed by four threads plaited, and the other four by threads twisted together; but these beautiful and costly grounds are now for ordinary purposes replaced by the fine machine-made net, so well known under the name of " Brussels net."

The Brussels flowers are of two kinds, those made with the needle, " point à l'aiguille," and those on the pillow, called " point plat ;" both are made distinct from the grounds.

In old Brussels lace the flowers were worked into the ground; the pillow-made or ". Brussels plat " are sewn on or " applied." The " modes " or " fillings " of Brussels lace are peculiarly beautiful, and it is also celebrated for the perfection of the relief or cordonnet which surrounds the flowers. The making of this exquisite lace is so complicated that each process is assigned to a separate hand who works only at her own department, knowing nothing of the general effect to be produced by the whole, the sole responsibility of which rests with the head of the establishment.

Brussels lace is still called in France by its old appellation of " point d'Angleterre," or " English point," a name to be explained by history. In 1662, the English Parliament, alarmed at the sums of money sent out of the country for the purchase of foreign lace, prohibited its importation. The English lace merchants, at a loss how to supply the Brussels lace required at the court of king Charles the second, and possessed of large funds, bought up all the choicest lace in Brussels and smuggled it over to England, where they produced it as " English point." To such an extent was this traffic carried on, that the name of " Brussels " lace became every day less known and was at last entirely usurped by that of " point d'Angleterre," which it retains even at the present time.

Mechlin is made in one piece on the pillow, and is the prettiest of laces. The ground is light and clear. Its distinguishing characteristic is the flat shining thread which forms the pattern and gives the appearance of embroidery. The manufacture has

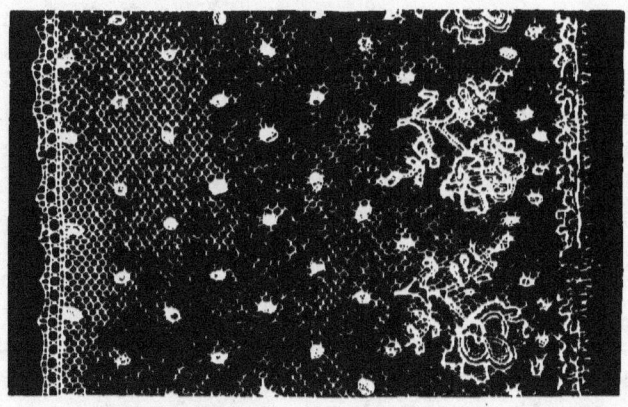

Border Lace, Mechlin; about 1800.

nearly died out. Mechlin lace has always held the highest favour in England.

West and east Flanders are the chief seats of the manufacture of Valenciennes lace, the art having been imported thither in the 17th century. It has attained the greatest perfection at Ypres (west Flanders), where it is made of the finest quality, and is remarkable for the large, clear, wire ground, the even tissue of its flowers, and its bold flowing patterns. Ypres makes the widest Valenciennes known; this is very costly, as high as 80*l.* the yard, but the making of such lace is very laborious; a lace-maker working 12 hours a day could scarcely produce one third of an inch a week, and as many as 1,200 bobbins are sometimes employed upon one pillow.

The art of making lace upon the pillow was first introduced into Germany by Barbara Etterlein, of Nuremberg parents, who removed to the mining district of the Hartz Mountains. Here she married a rich master miner, Christopher Uttmann of Annaberg. Observing that the girls were mostly employed in weaving net caps for the miners to confine their hair, Barbara, who had learned the art of lace-making from a Brabant refugee, introduced the pillow and taught them to make a plain lace ground, whence she proceeded to set up a workshop at Annaberg, and began to make lace of various patterns. Thence the art spread over Germany. Barbara Uttmann died at Annaberg, and on her tomb is incribed, " Here lies Barbara Uttmann, died 14 Jan. " 1575, whose invention of lace in the year 1561 made her the " benefactress of the Hartz mountains." This branch of industry, in which above 60,000 people were employed at the beginning of the present century, has greatly declined in the mountain district of the Erzgebirge, both on the Saxon and Bohemian sides, the peasants only making the coarse " torchon " lace. Machine-made lace has quite supplanted the hand-made, but great efforts have been lately made to revive the industry.

Lace-making is supposed to have been introduced into Denmark by queen Elizabeth, sister of the emperor Charles V., and wife of Christian II., but it has never been established as a manufacture except at Tönder in north Schleswig, whence lace was distributed over Scandinavia, by " lace postmen," as they were called. The old Tönder laces imitate the fabrics of the Netherlands, while the more modern were copied from the French, but the art has nearly died out.

The only manufactory of lace in Sweden is at the convent of Wadstena, founded by St. Bridget, and its products are carried to every part of the country by " colporteurs," or hawkers.

Much lace is made by the peasantry for their own use. The weaving of coarse pillow lace is the favourite occupation of the women of Scania, and in Dalecarlia the same patterns are used as were fabricated in other parts of Europe two centuries back. No improvement takes place in the designs, as the Dalecarlian women make only for their own consumption. The making of " Hölesom " or cutwork is a favourite occupation of the women in Sweden.

There is no established lace manufactory in Russia. The peasants bring their lace for sale to St. Petersburg. It is all of a coarse texture, the patterns of the same oriental character, and mostly used for church purposes.

France is the special country for lace. More is worn there than in all the rest of the world put together, and, of the lace-makers throughout Europe, one-half are estimated as belonging to France alone. The only needle-made lace is that of Alençon and Argentan, both towns in the department of the Orne. The principal pillow-made are those of Valenciennes, Lille, and Arras, with the various laces of Normandy, Auvergne, and Lorraine. Point d'Alençon is the only French lace not made on the pillow,

Lappet, 'point d'Alençon': eighteenth century.

except point d'Argentan, a fabric which of late years has been confounded with that of Alençon. The manufacture of Alençon was established by Colbert, the minister who gave the first impulse to the lace industry of France. He sent to Venice for lace-workers, and placed them in his own château near Alençon. But they could not succeed in teaching their French pupils to make the true Venetian stitches, so they struck into a new path, and invented a lace which was immediately adopted by Louis the fourteenth and his court. Alençon point is the most complicated and elaborate of all fabrics, being made entirely by hand with a needle on a parchment pattern, in small segments, each part executed by a different workwoman. So elaborate is its workmanship that a piece of lace formerly passed through 18 different hands before it was completed; the number is now reduced to 12.

The lace is thus made. The pattern is printed off on pieces of green parchment, about ten inches long, each segment numbered in its order; the pattern is then pricked through upon the parchment, which is next stitched to a piece of coarse linen folded double. The outline of the pattern is traced out by two threads fixed by small stitches, passed with another thread and needle, through the parchment and its linen lining. When the outline is finished the piece is given over to another worker to make the ground, which is worked backwards and forwards at right angles to the border. The flowers are next worked in; then follow the "modes" or "fillings," and other different operations. When completed, the threads which unite lace, parchment, and linen together are cut by passing a razor between the folds of the linen, and there remains only the great work of uniting the different segments together. This process devolves upon the head of the fabric, and is effected by the stitch called "assemblage;" by us termed "fine joining." Point d'Alençon is the only lace in which horse-hair is introduced along the edge, to give firmness and consistency to the "cordonnet."

From the labour expended in producing it point d'Alençon is the most costly of all lace. Fabulous are the sums that were lavished upon it in the last century, and a wedding order will even now sometimes amount to 6,000*l*.

'Point d'Argentan'; eighteenth century.

Argentan, near Alençon in the department of the Orne, is celebrated for its needle-made lace, established about the same time as Alençon, but, though often mistaken for such, there is an essential difference between the two fabrics, both in the flower and the ground. The flowers are heavier and more compact in point d'Argentan, retaining more of their Venetian character. The ground is of most elaborate workmanship, consisting of large hexagonal meshes, each side of which is worked over with the button-hole stitch, giving it extraordinary strength and solidity. The pattern is most effective on this clear large meshed ground, which is called "bride." Point d'Argentan perished with the French revolution, and all attempts to rediscover the manner of making it have proved unsuccessful. For many years its existence was forgotten, and it was held to be a coarse variety of point d'Alençon. Not long since, some magnificent flowers of point d'Argentan were seen by Mrs. Palliser which had been transferred to bobbin net, in order to get rid of its "ugly coarse ground."

Valenciennes lace dates from the 15th century. It flourished under Louis the fourteenth, reached its climax from 1725 to 1780, and fell with the monarchy, every effort to revive the manufacture having failed. The transfer of this industry to Belgium is a great commercial loss to France, as more is consumed of Valenciennes lace than of any other. Valenciennes lace is made entirely on the pillow, the same thread being used for both pattern and ground. In the ground all six sides of the mesh are plaited, which renders it the strongest and most durable of laces. Hence it was styled "eternal Valenciennes." So great was the labour of making it, that where a Lille lace-maker could produce three to five ells a day a Valenciennes worker could not accomplish more than an inch and a half. It took two months, working fifteen hours a day to complete a pair of ruffles. Valenciennes lace was therefore very costly. The city-made lace alone was called "real Valenciennes" (*vraie Valenciennes*), and was remarkable for the beauty of its ground, the richness of its design, and the evenness of its tissue.

A fine specimen of this lace of the period of Louis the fourteenth is in the museum, No. 550. The ground is fine and compact, the flower resembling cambric, and the design bold and florid; the truthfulness of the flowers showing its Flemish origin, for Valenciennes formed part of the ancient province of Hainault, and was only transferred to France by conquest and treaty at the end of the seventeenth century.

Lille lace equals in antiquity the laces of the Netherlands, of which country Lille, as Valenciennes, was anciently a part. The special excellence of Lille lace is its single ground; the finest, lightest, and most transparent known. Instead of the sides of the meshes being plaited, either partly as in Brussels or wholly as in Valenciennes, four of the sides are formed by twisting two threads round each other, and the remaining two sides by the simple crossing of the threads over each other. A thick thread marks the pattern. The edges of the old Lille lace are generally straight. The black was much worn for mantles, but it is now no longer made, and little is produced of the white. The lace of Arras resembles that of Lille in workmanship.

Chantilly, in the department of Oise, is the centre of a district long celebrated for its black and white silk laces, a manufacture established in the seventeenth century by the duchesse de Longueville. The flower and ground are of the same silk. Its productions being exclusively for the use of the higher classes, the lacemakers were many of them victims of the revolution. Under the first empire blonde lace again became worn, and Chantilly recovering its prosperity exported extensively to Spain and her American colonies mantillas, scarfs, and other large pieces, in the making of which she had no competitor. Later she has had to contend with the fabrics of Normandy, and her manufacture has succumbed in the contest. Chantilly at present fabricates none; she has been supplanted by the productions of Calvados, which are similar in material and in the mode of fabrication.

With the exception of the Valenciennes-making town of Bailleul the lace industry of France is now concentrated in the provinces of Normandy, Auvergne, and Lorraine. Alençon continues her world-wide celebrated point, which Bayeux now also makes. The Valenciennes and black lace manufacture extends from Cherbourg to Dieppe, and the last occupies the whole department of Calvados, for the white blondes of Caen have now yielded to machine-made imitations, though from the absence of brilliancy in the "grenadine" silk it is often called "black thread." Machine-made lace of low price is often made of black cotton, but never hand-made. The black lace, identical with Chantilly, has its centre at Bayeux, which town has arrived in its products at the highest point of artistic excellence. It is entirely made of silk.

Auvergne is one of the most ancient sites of the lace manufacture in France, and employs almost the whole female population. It produces every kind of lace, black and white, thread, cotton, silk, poil de chèvre, and woollen, the white thread like the old Lille and Arras. It formerly exported largely to Spain and its colonies. Le Puy and Crâponne, established in 1836, are the principal places of manufacture.

Lorraine, since the beginning of the last century, has carried on an extensive lace trade, but her productions have no special character of their own, Mirecourt (dépt. des Vosges) seeking rather to bring out novelties to meet the changes of fashion than to arrive at artistic excellence.

The introduction of pillow lace-making into England is assigned to the Netherlanders who fled from the persecutions of Alva, and sought an asylum on our shores. The two great centres of lace-making are Buckinghamshire and Honiton in Devonshire.

The laces of Buckinghamshire and the adjacent counties of Bedfordshire and Northampton are celebrated for the clearness and beauty of their "point" grounds, rivalling those of Lille.

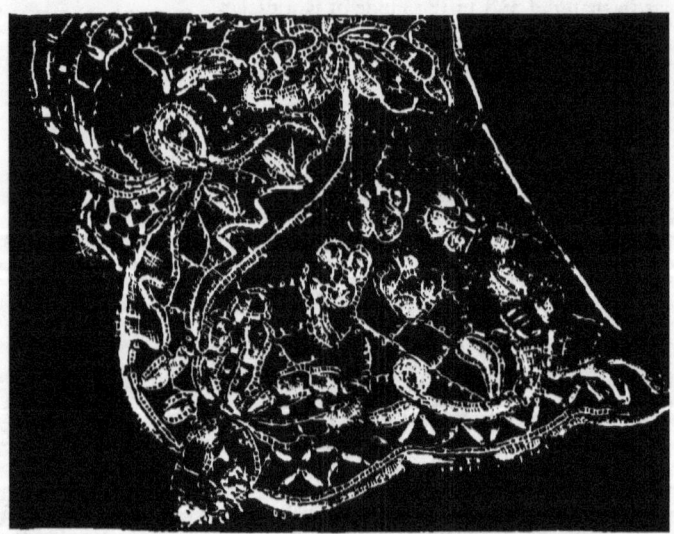

Honiton: modern.

whose patterns they copied; hence these laces have been called "English Lille." The principal branch of the trade was the making of those narrow laces specially employed for trimming infants' caps, called in the country where they are made "baby lace," but the discontinuance of the wearing of caps by infants and the increase of machine-made lace have caused the demand for these laces to decline, and the lace-makers have given up their Lille grounds, and make Cluny and Maltese lace.

The lace manufacture of Devonshire extends along the sea-coast from Seaton by Beer, Branscombe, and Sidmouth, to Exmouth, including the vale of Honiton which is its chief centre. The Honiton lace resembles the Brussels in manufacture. The old ground was beautifully fine and regular, made of thread procured at Antwerp, where its market price in 1790 was 70*l*. the lb., as high as a hundred guineas having been paid for it to smugglers during the war; and the lace-makers would receive as much as 18*s*. the yard for making the ground of border lace, not two inches wide. But it is to its sprigs that Honiton owes its

Irish point: modern.

great reputation. They are made separately on the pillow, and like those of Brussels were at first worked in and afterwards "applied" or sewn on the ground.

Honiton lace was very costly ; a veil would be worth a hundred guineas. Honiton workers still retain their celebrity for the excellence of their work, but the style is altered, and the fine ground and delicate sprigs which made them famous have been replaced by the modern "guipure."

It was through the patriotic exertions of the Lady Arabella Denny, in the middle of the last century, that the art of lace-making was taught to the children in the workhouse at Dublin, and, after the great famine of 1846, various lace schools were set up in different parts of Ireland, where lace was made with great success. Lady de Vere taught the art of making application flowers like Brussels, called from her demesne in the county of Limerick "Curragh point." Irish guipure was made at Carrickmacross, county of Monaghan ; imitation of ancient point, at Miss Jane Clarke's school at Belfast ; Valenciennes of Ypres, at Lady Erne's, county Fermanagh, with "lacet," tatting, and various other descriptions of lace of admirable finish.

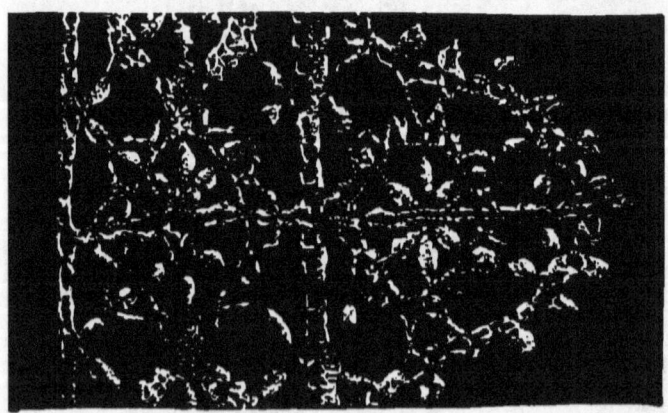

Genoese point ; sixteenth century.

www.ingramcontent.com/pod-product-compliance
Lightning Source LLC
Chambersburg PA
CBHW032057220426
43664CB00008B/1044